DON'T LET DOUBT TAKE YOU OUT

Winning Strategies to Manage Doubt, Overcome Fear, Build Confidence, And Create an Unstoppable Life

JERRY ROISENTUL

JERRY ROISENTUL

Printed Worldwide
First Printing 2023
First Edition 2023

ISBN: 979-8863316307

10 9 8 7 6 5 4 3 2 1

Editor - Josh Griswold

DON'T LET DOUBT
TAKE YOU OUT

DEDICATION

First and foremost, I dedicate this book to my heavenly father, who saved me so many years ago from taking my life. I wouldn't be who I am or where I am today without him. He lifted me out of the pit of despair, out of the mud and the mire. He set my feet on solid ground and steadied me as I walked. He has given me a new song to sing, a hymn of praise to our God. Many will see what he has done and be amazed, and they will put their trust in the Lord. I honor God today with this book.

I dedicate this book to my Dad, who I know is smiling down from heaven. I learned so much about being an entrepreneur and a father from him. He would be so proud of me knowing I finally wrote the book I have been talking about writing for over 30 years. I love and miss you dad.

To my mom: my biggest fan and cheerleader. Thank you for all the love, support, and encouragement you have always given me. I wouldn't be the man I am without you.

To my son: Being your dad and watching you grow into a young man has been the greatest joy of my life. Let this book be an example to you to never give up on your dreams. No matter how long it may take, you persevere until you get it done. I could not imagine my life without you.

To my immediate family: My brother Gary, Sister-in-Law Diana, and my niece Kaylin: I love you all so much and am grateful to share this journey with you. Thank you for your love and support.

To all of my coaching clients over the last ten years: There is way too many of you to name, but you all know who you are. We have shared laughs, tears, victories, failures, and successes. You have added as much value to my life as I hope I have to yours. All of you are a small part of this book.

And to my extended family and friends…thank you for being a light in my life. I couldn't imagine life without you.

TABLE OF CONTENTS

INTRODUCTION

Congratulations! You've taken the first step towards transforming your life and business by investing in the book "Don't Let Doubt Take You Out: Winning Strategies to Manage Doubt, Overcome Fear, Build Confidence, and Create an Unstoppable Life." You hold within your hands a powerful tool that will guide you on your journey to conquer doubt and fear and achieve the success you desire as an entrepreneur.

In this book, Jerry Roisentul, a renowned Keynote Speaker, Maxwell Leadership Certified Coach and Trainer, as well as a Certified Behavioral Analysis Consultant, shares practical advice, tips, case studies, and real-life examples to help you master the art of managing doubt, overcoming fear, and building unshakeable confidence. Through his wealth of experience and expertise, he aims to provide you with the tools and strategies necessary to overcome self-doubt, cultivate lasting confidence, and manage their mindset effectively.

Why Overcoming Doubt and Fear Matters:

As an entrepreneur, doubt and fear can be debilitating, posing significant barriers to your success. The constant internal battle between your ambitions and the negative thoughts can demoralize you, hinder progress, and drain your belief in yourself. The good news is that by implementing the strategies outlined in this book, you will learn how to embrace doubt and fear as catalysts for growth rather than roadblocks.

Building Confidence and Managing Your Mindset:

Jerry takes you on a transformative journey, helping you explore the root causes of your doubts and fears. Through inspirational storytelling and a conversational writing style, he shares relatable experiences that illustrate powerful strategies for building unwavering confidence. By understanding yourself better and discovering your strengths, you will be equipped to navigate the challenges of entrepreneurship with resilience and courage.

Practical Advice and Strategies:

This book is your trusted companion, offering practical advice, tips, tricks, and actionable strategies that you can apply immediately to your life and business. Jerry draws on his practical knowledge gained from coaching and training countless entrepreneurs like yourself, empowering you with the tools you need to overcome obstacles and move past self-doubt swiftly.

Maximizing the Power of This Book:

As you delve deep into the pages of "Don't Let Doubt Take You Out," it's important to approach each chapter with an open mind and a willingness to challenge your limiting beliefs. Embrace the friendly and conversational tone in which the concepts are presented, allowing yourself to truly absorb the invaluable insights provided. Remember, the purpose of this book is to guide you towards creating an unstoppable life, and to do so, you must be engaged and proactive in applying the strategies in your own journey.

Conclusion:

By the time you finish reading this book, you'll have gained the knowledge and confidence to manage your mindset effectively, reshape your thoughts, and respond to doubts and fears with unwavering resolve. "Don't Let Doubt Take You Out" is not just a guide, but a stepping stone towards achieving your wildest dreams.

Remember, you have the ability to overcome doubt, conquer fears, and build the unstoppable life you desire. Now, it's time to embark on this transformative journey and unlock the vast potential within you. Start reading the book in your hands and allow Jerry to be your steadfast guide as you embark on this empowering transformation. The power to succeed is within you; it's time to unleash it!

CHAPTER 1

FROM DOUBT TO TRIUMPH: MY JOURNEY OF OVERCOMING FEAR, CONQUERING DOUBT, & TRANSFORMING MY MINDSET

In this chapter, we will cover how to:

- Overcoming doubt and fear: Learn how to transform your mindset and conquer negative emotions that hold you back.

- Embracing uncertainty: Discover the power of taking calculated risks and stepping outside your comfort zone for personal and professional growth.

- Building a supportive network: Surround yourself with like-minded individuals who understand your struggles and can provide encouragement and empowerment.

- Reframing negative thoughts: Find out how positive affirmations, visualizations, and motivational resources can help maintain a positive mindset and fuel your inspiration.

My journey in overcoming doubt and fear and transforming my mindset has been a rollercoaster ride filled with valuable lessons and significant growth.

Like many entrepreneurial professionals, I have faced countless moments of self-doubt and fear throughout my career. There were times when I questioned my abilities and felt overwhelmed by the challenges ahead.

But instead of letting these negative emotions consume me, I consciously confronted them head-on and transformed my mindset.

One pivotal moment in my journey was realizing that doubt and fear are natural parts of the process. They are not indicators of failure or incompetence but stepping stones towards growth and success. I started viewing doubt as an opportunity to learn and improve and fear as a sign that I was pushing myself out of my comfort zone.

To conquer doubt, I began focusing on my strengths and achievements. I started by making a list of my accomplishments, big and small, to remind myself of the progress I had already made. I sought feedback from trusted mentors and peers, allowing their perspectives to neutralize my doubts.

I also surrounded myself with a supportive network of like-minded individuals who understood my struggles. I gained camaraderie and encouragement by building relationships with people who shared similar goals and aspirations. Together, we formed a support system that propelled us forward when doubt and fear threatened to hold us back.

Transforming my mindset required a conscious effort to reframe negative thoughts and beliefs. I practiced positive affirmations and visualizations, consistently reminding myself of my capabilities and potential. I sought motivational resources like books, podcasts, and seminars to fuel my inspiration and maintain a positive mindset.

Additionally, I recognized the importance of taking calculated risks. I understood that growth lies outside my comfort zone, and I needed to embrace uncertainty and the possibility of failure.

I gradually built resilience and confidence by pushing myself to step into uncomfortable situations and confront my fears.

Ultimately, my journey in overcoming doubt and fear and transforming my mindset is ongoing. By adopting a positive and proactive approach, I have experienced tremendous growth and achieved milestones I once deemed impossible.

Let me tell you a quick story of how I overcame doubt in one of the most challenging endeavors in my life.

In 2011, I faced a daunting challenge when a friend asked me to do a training session for her team at a leadership meeting. Despite my lack of experience in coaching, my friend suggested I offer a 45-minute coaching session to the 30 individuals in attendance for just $20. Initially, I was confused, thinking, "Who would want to coach with me after meeting me for just 45 minutes?" However, to my surprise, 15 people accepted the offer. Panic set in as I realized I had no training materials, no courses, no clue.

To cope with the overwhelming doubt I began to feel, I personified it by giving it a name – Dan Doubt. (You can also call it Debbie Doubt if you'd like, but this just worked for me.) With my first coaching session on the horizon, I desperately needed to rush through it before my clients realized I had no idea what I was doing. That first client not only signed up for a six-month coaching program but also brought in several more clients. This sudden success amplified my doubt, as I questioned how I would sustain such momentum for six whole months. Dan Doubt reveled in this uncertainty, bombarding me with thoughts of failure, embarrassment, and destroying my reputation.

However, the story did not end there. Out of the first ten people I coached, eight of them signed up for extended coaching. Overwhelmed and feeling over my head, I turned to the strategies I had learned and applied throughout my journey. By managing my doubt, taking action despite my fear, and continuously implementing the tools outlined in this book, I could overcome the doubts I faced every day. This experience became the catalyst for building an international coaching business and traveling worldwide, sharing these principles with business leaders and entrepreneurs.

My testimony is an encouragement to anyone who may doubt their abilities. If I can overcome doubt and achieve success, so can you. Remember, doubt and fear are not roadblocks but opportunities for growth and success. Embrace the challenges, persist in the face of doubt, and watch as your endeavors flourish.

Now that I've shared a little of my journey, let's dive into a detailed case study that further illustrates the power of these strategies in transforming an individual's mindset and ultimately leading to success in the entrepreneurial world.

Case Study

Background:

John is an aspiring entrepreneur who has faced numerous moments of self-doubt and fear throughout his career. He often questioned his abilities and felt overwhelmed by the challenges ahead. However, he consciously confronted these negative emotions head-on and transformed his mindset.

Actions Taken:

1. **Reframing negative thoughts:** John started viewing doubt as an opportunity to learn and improve and fear as a sign of pushing himself out of his comfort zone. He practiced positive affirmations and visualizations to remind himself of his capabilities and potential.

2. **Focusing on strengths and achievements:** John made a list of his accomplishments, big and small, to remind himself of the progress he had already made. He sought feedback from trusted mentors and peers to neutralize his doubts.

3. **Building a supportive network:** John surrounded himself with like-minded individuals who understood his struggles. By forming relationships with people who shared similar goals and aspirations, he gained a sense of camaraderie and encouragement.

4. **Seeking motivational resources:** John actively sought motivational resources, such as books, podcasts, and seminars, to fuel his inspiration and maintain a positive mindset.

5. **Embracing discomfort and taking risks:** John recognized the importance of stepping outside his comfort zone. He pushed himself to confront his fears and embrace uncertainty, gradually building resilience and confidence.

Measurable Outcomes:

1. **Increased confidence:** John's consistent efforts to reframe negative thoughts and focus on his achievements significantly increased his confidence levels.

2. Milestone achievement: By adopting a positive and proactive approach, John achieved milestones he once deemed impossible in his entrepreneurial journey.

Challenges Faced:

1. Overcoming self-doubt: John faced the challenge of overcoming deep-rooted self-doubt, which required consistent self-reflection, personal development, and perseverance.

2. Embracing discomfort: Stepping outside his comfort zone was challenging for John, as it meant facing uncertainty and the possibility of failure. However, through gradual exposure to uncomfortable situations, he overcame this challenge.

Lessons Learned:

1. Doubt and fear are natural parts of the entrepreneurial journey: John realized that doubt and fear are not indicators of failure or incompetence but stepping stones toward growth and success.

2. Building a support system is crucial: Surrounding oneself with a supportive network of like-minded individuals who understand the struggles and aspirations can provide the necessary encouragement and motivation.

Assessment:

The strategies and principles implemented by John have proven successful in overcoming doubt and fear in entrepreneurship. By sharing his experience and providing guidance and support, he inspires others to build the confidence necessary to achieve their entrepreneurial goals.

John's case study demonstrates that the right mindset and support system can conquer self-doubt and fear and achieve remarkable success.

Now that we have explored John's journey of overcoming doubt and fear in entrepreneurship let's look at some critical mistakes to avoid building confidence and succeed in your entrepreneurial endeavors.

Typical Mistakes And How To Avoid Them

1. **Viewing doubt and fear as indicators of failure or incompetence**: Many people mistakenly believe that feeling doubt or fear means they are incapable or worthy of success. To avoid this mistake, remember that doubt and fear are natural parts of the process and can be stepping stones towards growth and success.

2. **Not focusing on strengths and achievements:** People often get caught up in their doubts and fears and forget to acknowledge their strengths and past accomplishments. To avoid this mistake, it is helpful to make a list of accomplishments, big and small, and regularly remind oneself of the progress already made.

3. **Not seeking feedback and support**: Some individuals try to overcome doubt and fear independently without seeking the input and help of trusted mentors and peers. To avoid this mistake, seeking feedback from those who have experience and understanding is beneficial, as their perspectives can help neutralize doubts.

4. **Not surrounding oneself with a supportive network:** Many underestimate the power of surrounding themselves with like-

minded individuals who understand their struggles. To avoid this mistake, building relationships with people who share similar goals and aspirations is important, forming a support system that propels everyone forward.

5. **Not practicing positive affirmations and visualizations:** People often neglect the importance of actively reframing negative thoughts and beliefs. To avoid this mistake, it is helpful to consistently practice positive affirmations and visualizations to remind oneself of capabilities and potential.

6. **Avoiding calculated risks and staying within comfort zones**: Many individuals fear taking risks and avoiding stepping outside their comfort zones, hindering their growth and development. To avoid this mistake, it is crucial to embrace uncertainty and the possibility of failure, understanding that growth lies outside of comfort zones.

Overall, it is essential to remember that overcoming doubt and fear is an ongoing process. By avoiding these common mistakes and adopting a positive and proactive approach, it is possible to achieve personal growth and entrepreneurial success.

With these common mistakes to avoid in mind, it is now crucial to introduce the #1 piece of advice that can help individuals overcome doubt and fear and ultimately achieve personal growth and success.

My #1 Piece Of Advice

Embrace failure as a stepping stone, not a setback. Learn from your mistakes and push through doubt and fear to grow personally and professionally.

I invite you to look at the checklist I have created. It outlines the strategies and principles discussed in this chapter that have helped me build confidence and achieve my goals. By implementing these strategies and seeking support, you can conquer doubt and fear and achieve greatness in your entrepreneurial journey.

<u>Action Steps Checklist</u>:

1. Make a list of your strengths and accomplishments to remind yourself of your progress.

2. Seek feedback from trusted mentors and peers to neutralize doubts.

3. Surround yourself with a supportive network of like-minded individuals who understand your struggles.

4. Practice positive affirmations and visualizations to reframe negative thoughts and beliefs.

5. Utilize motivational resources such as books, podcasts, and seminars to maintain a positive mindset.

6. Embrace uncertainty and take calculated risks to push yourself outside your comfort zone.

7. Engage in continuous self-reflection and personal development to fuel growth.

8. Seek guidance and support from mentors and like-minded individuals.

9. Embrace doubt and fear as opportunities for growth and success.

10. Believe in your capabilities and potential to achieve your entrepreneurial goals.

The most compelling aspect of my journey was discovering how specific techniques and exercises played a crucial role in silencing my inner doubts and fears, paving the way for a transformative mindset. If you're seeking practical tools to quiet that negative voice and cultivate a more positive outlook, let's delve into the next chapter, where I'll share some invaluable techniques that can help you on your path toward success."

CHAPTER 2

SILENCE THE DOUBT: POWERFUL STRATEGIES TO MASTER YOUR MINDSET AND CRUSH NEGATIVE THOUGHTS

"In life, you learn to manage your mindset, or your mindset will manage you." – Jerry Roisentul

In this chapter, we will cover how to:

- Discover how entrepreneurs can effectively manage their mindset in challenging times and high-pressure situations.
- Learn the power of mindfulness in reducing stress and enhancing focus for entrepreneurs.
- Uncover the techniques of using affirmations and positive self-talk to reframe negative thoughts.
- Explore the practice of cognitive restructuring to shift mindset towards a more positive and growth-oriented perspective.
- Find out how gratitude practice, visualization, and mental rehearsal can help entrepreneurs overcome doubts and fears.

Overcoming the negative voice in one's head and fostering a positive mindset is crucial for entrepreneurs, especially in challenging times or high-pressure situations.

To effectively manage your mindset, you can employ several techniques and exercises that have proven effective. Here are some specific strategies you can utilize:

1. **Mindfulness and Quiet Time**: These practices can help you understand your thoughts and emotions. By bringing attention to the present moment and observing your negative thoughts without judgment, you can gradually detach from them and create space for more positive and constructive thinking. Regular mindfulness and quiet time practices have been shown to reduce stress, enhance focus, and improve overall well-being.

2. **Affirmations and Positive Self-Talk**: Encouraging positive self-talk and repeating affirmations can be powerful tools to reframe negative thoughts. You can create a list of empowering affirmations aligned with your goals, strengths, and values. By consistently repeating these affirmations and incorporating positive self-talk throughout the day, you can challenge and replace the negative voice in your head with more constructive and supportive messages. I will share more on this topic in a later chapter.

3. **Cognitive Restructuring**: This technique involves identifying and reevaluating negative thoughts and beliefs. You can start by recognizing negative self-talk patterns and actively questioning their validity. They can challenge the accuracy of negative thoughts, evaluate evidence for and against them, and generate more realistic and optimistic alternatives. By consciously rewiring your thinking, you can gradually shift your mindset towards a more positive and growth-oriented perspective.

4. **Gratitude Practice**: Cultivating a gratitude practice can help you redirect your focus toward the positive aspects of your life and business. Every day, you can list or reflect upon things you are grateful for, including achievements, supportive relationships, or personal growth. This exercise helps develop a mindset of abundance and appreciation, counteracting the tendency to dwell on negative thoughts or setbacks.

5. **Visualization and Mental Rehearsal**: Visualization techniques can help create a clear and compelling mental image of your desired outcomes. By repeatedly visualizing yourself successfully navigating challenging situations, you can enhance your confidence and develop a belief in your abilities. Additionally, mental rehearsal involves practicing actions, responses, and problem-solving strategies, making you feel more prepared and less overwhelmed during high-pressure situations.

Entrepreneurs like yourself must understand that these techniques require consistent practice and dedication to yield long-term results. By incorporating these exercises into their daily routine and committing to their implementation, you can gradually quiet the negative voice in your head and cultivate a more positive and resilient mindset, enabling you to overcome doubts and fears effectively.

By using these techniques consistently and integrating them into their daily routine, you can learn to quiet their negative inner voice and cultivate a positive mindset that supports their success and well-being.

Now, let's explore a case study that further illustrates the power of these strategies and how they work in a real-world situation. As you read this, ask yourself how you can apply these principles to your life and business.

Case Study

Background:

ABC Corporation is a technology startup founded by Sarah, an ambitious entrepreneur with a solid drive to succeed. However, Sarah often overwhelms herself with negative thoughts and self-doubt, especially during challenging times or high-pressure situations. Recognizing the importance of managing her mindset, she implements a series of strategies to overcome these obstacles and foster a positive attitude.

Implementation:

1. **Mindfulness and Quiet Time**: Sarah practices these techniques for 15 minutes every morning. By focusing on her breath and observing her thoughts without judgment, she becomes more aware of her negative thinking patterns and learns to detach from them. Over time, she noticed a decrease in stress levels and an improvement in her ability to stay focused.

2. **Affirmations and Positive Self-Talk**: Sarah creates a list of empowering affirmations that align with her goals and values. She repeats these affirmations throughout the day and incorporates positive self-talk into her daily routine. By challenging and replacing negative thoughts with more constructive messages, she notices a shift in her mindset, feeling more confident and optimistic.

3. **Cognitive Restructuring**: Sarah actively identifies her negative self-talk patterns and questions their validity. She evaluates the evidence for and against her negative thoughts, generating more realistic and optimistic alternatives. Through this process, she gradually rewires her thinking and develops a more positive and growth-oriented perspective.

4. **Gratitude Practice**: Sarah starts a gratitude journal, listing three things she is grateful for at the end of each day. This exercise helps her redirect her focus towards the positive aspects of her life and business. By cultivating a mindset of abundance and appreciation, she becomes less prone to dwelling on negative thoughts or setbacks.

5. **Visualization and Mental Rehearsal**: Sarah incorporates visualization techniques into her daily routine. She spends a few minutes daily visualizing herself successfully navigating challenging situations and achieving her goals. Additionally, she mentally rehearses actions, responses, and problem-solving strategies, which helps her feel more prepared and less overwhelmed during high-pressure situations.

Outcomes:

After several months of consistently practicing these strategies, Sarah experiences measurable outcomes in managing her mindset:

1. **Improved Confidence**: Sarah's confidence levels significantly increased, allowing her to take risks and handle challenges more effectively.

2. **Enhanced Focus**: By reducing her self-doubt and replacing it with positive thinking, Sarah finds it easier to stay focused on her goals and tasks.

3. **Reduced Stress**: Regular mindfulness and meditation practices have helped Sarah reduce her stress levels, improving her overall well-being

Lessons Learned:

Through this experience, Sarah learned the following lessons:

1. **Consistency is Key**: Regular and consistent practice is essential for these techniques to bring about lasting changes in mindset.

2. **Be Patient**: Overcoming negative self-talk and cultivating a positive mindset requires time and patience. It's essential to trust the process and not expect immediate results.

Overall Impact:

The implementation of these strategies had a significant impact on Sarah's ability to manage her mindset effectively:

1. **Improved Resilience**: Sarah becomes more resilient in facing challenges overcoming doubts and fears more effectively.

2. **Enhanced Decision-Making**: By shifting her mindset towards positivity and growth, Sarah's decision-making abilities improve, leading to better outcomes for her business.

3. **Positive Work Environment**: Sarah's positive mindset influences her team, creating a more supportive and collaborative work environment.

In conclusion, by consistently implementing these tools, Sarah successfully manages her mindset, allowing her to overcome challenges and achieve her goals. This case study exemplifies the critical information and points discussed in this chapter, highlighting specific actions taken, measurable outcomes achieved, lessons learned, and the overall impact on Sarah's ability to manage her mindset effectively.

Now that we have explored Sarah's journey in overcoming negative self-talk and cultivating a positive mindset let's take a closer look at some common mistakes to avoid when implementing these strategies.

Typical Mistakes And How To Avoid Them

1. **Not being aware of negative thoughts:** Many tend to let negative thoughts consume them without realizing it. By being aware of your thoughts and emotions, you can identify negative patterns and actively work to detach from them.

2. **Not challenging negative self-talk:** People often listen to their negative inner voice without questioning its validity. Instead, it would help if you actively challenged negative thoughts and beliefs. By examining the accuracy of these thoughts and generating more realistic alternatives, you can reframe your mindset in a positive and growth-oriented way.

3. **Lacking gratitude and appreciation:** Focusing on negative thoughts and setbacks can make it difficult to see the good in life and business. Cultivating a gratitude practice can help shift the focus towards the positive aspects. Taking time each day to reflect

on what you are grateful for can counteract the tendency to dwell on negativity.

4. **Inconsistent practice**: These techniques require regular practice and dedication to see long-term results. Many people may try them for a short period of time and then give up. To avoid this, you should commit to incorporating these exercises into your daily routine and consistently implement them.

5. **Lack of visualization and mental rehearsal**: Many people need to pay more attention to the power of visualizing success and mentally rehearsing challenging situations. By regularly visualizing themselves overcoming obstacles and practicing problem-solving strategies in their mind, you can enhance your confidence and belief in your abilities.

By being aware of these common mistakes and actively working to avoid them, you can effectively manage your mindset and foster a positive approach to overcoming doubts and fears in challenging times.

Now that we have identified the common mistakes to avoid in managing one's mindset, it is vital to introduce the #1 piece of advice to help entrepreneurs overcome these challenges.

My #1 Piece Of Advice

You can't always control the doubts and fears that will come against your mind, but you have total control over which ones you will let in and focus on. Don't give doubt and fear an open door in your mind to come in. Use the tools in this chapter to keep them out.

As we wrap up this chapter, let's look at a powerful Action Steps checklist I have created to help you implement these techniques into your daily routine. Remember that repetition is the mother of learning.

Action Steps Checklist:

1. **Start a regular mindfulness and quiet time practice:**

 - Set aside a specific time each day.

 - Find a quiet and comfortable space to practice.

 - Focus on your breath and bring your attention to the present moment.

 - Observe your thoughts and emotions without judgment.

 - Gradually detach from negative thoughts and create space for positive thinking.

2. **Create a list of empowering affirmations:**

 - Identify your goals, strengths, and values.

 - Formulate positive affirmations that align with these aspects.

 - Repeat these affirmations consistently throughout the day.

 - Incorporate positive self-talk into your daily routine.

3. **Practice cognitive restructuring:**

 - Recognize negative self-talk patterns.

 - Question the validity and accuracy of negative thoughts.

 - Generate realistic and optimistic alternatives.

 - Challenge negative beliefs and rewire your thinking.

4. **Cultivate a gratitude practice**:

- Set aside time daily to reflect on things you are grateful for.

- Write down or mentally acknowledge these things.

- Focus on achievements, supportive relationships, and personal growth.

- Shift your focus from negative thoughts to appreciate the positive aspects of your life and business.

5. **Utilize visualization and mental rehearsal techniques**:

- Visualize yourself successfully navigating challenging situations.

- Create a clear and compelling mental image of your desired outcomes.

- Repeat this visualization practice regularly.

- Engage in mental rehearsal by practicing actions, responses, and problem-solving strategies.

Remember, consistent practice and dedication are crucial for long-term results. Commit to incorporating these exercises into your daily routine and prioritize their implementation. Over time, you will quiet the negative voice in your head and cultivate a more positive and resilient mindset as an entrepreneur.

Now that we've explored various techniques to quiet that negative voice in your head, it's time to delve into another crucial aspect of your entrepreneurial journey - recognizing and overcoming limiting beliefs hindering your progress. Keep reading to discover practical strategies that will empower you to push past your self-imposed limitations and unlock your true potential!

CHAPTER 3

BREAKING THE CHAINS: HOW TO OVERCOME THE LIMITING BELIEFS THAT ARE HOLDING YOU BACK FROM SUCCESS

"We learn our belief systems as tiny children, and then we move through life creating experiences to match our beliefs." Louise L Hay.

In this chapter, we will cover how to:

- Discover how past experiences can create a mental framework that reinforces self-doubt and limits your true potential as an entrepreneur.

- Uncover the societal conditioning that may be holding you back and learn how to challenge these norms to redefine your potential for success.

- Take actionable steps like identifying and challenging your limiting beliefs, reframing negative experiences, and surrounding yourself with positive influences to overcome doubt and achieve your goals.

- Embrace a growth mindset that sees challenges as opportunities for growth and believes in your ability to develop skills and intelligence through dedication and hard work.

- Learn how to set achievable goals, track your progress, practice positive affirmations, and commit to lifelong learning to improve and cultivate the confidence needed for entrepreneurial success continually.

My definition of a limiting belief is simple: It is a negative belief that **WE'VE** created in our mind that we **REINFORCE** by thinking, speaking, and focusing on it. And by doing so, it limits us from taking action that will help us accomplish our goals.

Limiting beliefs are formed through a complex interplay of various factors, such as past experiences, societal conditioning, and personal perceptions. Understanding how these beliefs are formed is crucial for entrepreneurs who want to overcome them and eliminate doubt from their mindset effectively.

First and foremost, they often stem from past experiences that hurt us. These experiences could be personal failures, rejections, or even criticisms from others. Such experiences create a mental framework that reinforces self-doubt and instills the belief that similar outcomes will occur in the future. It would be best to recognize that these beliefs are often based on distorted perceptions of reality and may not accurately represent their true capabilities.

Additionally, societal conditioning plays a significant role in shaping limiting beliefs. Throughout our lives, we are exposed to various societal norms and expectations, which can mold our ideas about what is achievable and what is not. Cultural and social influences can lead us to doubt their abilities, often making them feel trapped in a predetermined set of limitations. You must challenge these societal norms and redefine your potential.

To effectively overcome limiting beliefs, you must employ a multifaceted approach combining self-reflection, reprogramming thought patterns, and adopting supportive strategies. Here are a few key steps that you can take:

1. **Identify and challenge limiting beliefs**: Start by identifying the specific beliefs holding you back. Question their validity and challenge the evidence that supports them. Recognize that many of these beliefs are irrational and not based on facts.

I have learned that limiting beliefs generally hide in areas where you're producing results you don't want.

2. **Reframe negative experiences**: Reinterpret past failures or rejections as learning experiences rather than confirmation of inability. Understand that failure is a natural part of the entrepreneurial journey and does not define one's potential for success.

3. **Surround yourself with positive influences**: Seek mentors, coaches, and like-minded individuals who can provide support, guidance, and encouragement. Surrounding yourself with positive influences can help to counteract the negative beliefs that arise from self-doubt.

4. **Foster a growth mindset**: Embrace the belief that abilities and knowledge can be developed through dedication and hard work. Cultivate an attitude that sees challenges as opportunities for growth rather than obstacles.

5. **Set achievable goals and track progress**: Break down larger goals into smaller, manageable tasks. By setting achievable milestones and tracking progress, entrepreneurs can boost their confidence and reinforce their belief in their ability to succeed.

6. **Continual self-improvement**: Commit to lifelong learning and personal development. Enhancing skills and knowledge will boost

confidence and provide entrepreneurs with tangible evidence of their abilities.

In summary, overcoming limiting beliefs requires consciously challenging and replacing negative thoughts with positive and empowering beliefs. By following these strategies, you can effectively overcome doubt and cultivate the confidence needed to succeed.

Here are a few examples of how limiting beliefs show up in different scenarios:

Examples

Example of a limiting belief formed from past experiences: A person who was repeatedly told they were not artistic growing up may develop a belief that they have no artistic abilities. This may hinder them from pursuing creative endeavors later in life.

Example of a limiting belief shaped by societal conditioning: In certain cultures, there may be a strong emphasis on stability and security, leading individuals to believe that taking risks or starting their own business is too risky or unrealistic.

Example of challenging and reframing a limiting belief: An entrepreneur who experienced a business failure may initially believe they are not cut out for entrepreneurship. However, they can reframe this experience as a valuable learning opportunity and understand that failure is a natural part of the entrepreneurial journey.

Example of seeking positive influences: An entrepreneur lacking confidence in their abilities may seek a mentor who has achieved success in their field. This mentor can provide guidance, support, and encouragement, helping them challenge and overcome their limiting beliefs.

Example of fostering a growth mindset: Entrepreneurs who believe their knowledge and abilities are fixed may struggle to overcome challenges. By embracing a growth mindset, they can cultivate the belief that they can develop their skills through dedication and hard work.

Example of practicing positive affirmations and visualization: Entrepreneurs who constantly doubt their abilities may use positive affirmations to reprogram their subconscious mind. They may repeat statements such as "I am capable of achieving greatness" to reinforce positive beliefs and visualize themselves overcoming challenges and achieving success.

Example of continual self-improvement: An entrepreneur who desires to overcome limiting beliefs may commit to lifelong learning and personal development. They may attend workshops, take courses, and actively seek opportunities to enhance their skills and knowledge, providing tangible evidence of their capabilities and boosting their confidence.

Now that we have explored various examples of limiting beliefs and strategies for overcoming them let's delve into a case study that illustrates the transformative power of challenging and overcoming limiting beliefs.

Usually, the case study will be about someone who has applied these principles to their business and made a fantastic turnaround. But today, the case study is about someone you know personally: ME!

<u>Case Study</u>

I am going to share a very personal story with you to show you how you do not have to be a victim of your limiting beliefs. It is a journey of overcoming the damaging words that held me back for so long.

When I was about 6 or 7, I used to love working in the garden with my dad. It was a special bonding time for us, and I cherished those moments. However, this is also where my limiting beliefs were formed. He would always ask me to go to the garage and get a tool, he would describe. However, with a wall filled with tools, I often needed help finding the right one.

This led to moments of frustration for my dad. He would come in, pull the tool off the wall, and say hurtful things like, "Are you Blind? Are you dumb? Stupid? An imbecile?" My dad didn't realize the power of his words and the potential damage they could cause. Despite his love for me and our close relationship, he unknowingly treated me as if he might have been treated as a child.

As I grew up, I carried those limiting beliefs around with me. They became ingrained in my mind and influenced how I viewed myself. One defining moment occurred in middle school when the teacher asked us what we wanted to be when we grew up. Hearing my friends enthusiastically share their dreams, I couldn't help but feel inadequate. When it was my turn, I responded, "Whatever a dumb, stupid imbecile can do."

The shock on the teacher's face and the reaction from my friends made me realize how deeply these beliefs were affecting me. It was a wake-up call that forced me to make a choice. Let those thoughts continue to limit me, or I could create new beliefs that would empower me and allow me to reach my full potential.

Taking to heart the principles I am sharing with you in this chapter, I embarked on a journey of self-discovery. With great compassion, I identified my limiting beliefs and reframed them into empowering beliefs. I consciously surrounded myself with people who would encourage and support these new beliefs. Personal development became my constant companion as I committed to grow and evolve.

Through this process, I transformed the direction of my life. I realized that my past did not define me, and I could rise above the limitations I had carried for far too long. Without that experience, I could not teach you the principles that have enabled me to overcome my limiting beliefs and truly thrive.

By sharing my testimony, you, too, can find the strength and resilience to overcome any limiting beliefs that may be holding you back. You have the power within you to break free from the shackles of the past and embrace a future full of limitless opportunities.

Remember, you are the author of your story, and no one else gets to write the script for you. By embracing your worth, challenging your limiting beliefs, and taking consistent action toward your goals, you can overcome any obstacle that comes your way. Believe in yourself and know you have the strength and resilience to rise above any challenge. Your past does not define you, but it can be the catalyst for your personal growth and transformation. Embrace your journey and know that you can achieve greatness.

Now that we have examined my journey of overcoming limiting beliefs that almost changed the direction of my life, it is essential to identify and discuss the critical mistakes to avoid that can hinder the progress of aspiring entrepreneurs.

Typical Mistakes And How To Avoid Them

One common mistake most people make is not recognizing that their limiting beliefs are often based on distorted perceptions of reality. When we experience past failures or criticisms from others, it can create a mental framework that reinforces self-doubt. However, it's important to question the validity of these beliefs and challenge the evidence that supports them.

Another mistake is allowing societal conditioning to shape our beliefs about what is achievable. We are constantly exposed to societal norms and expectations, leading us to doubt our abilities and feel trapped in a predetermined set of limitations. To avoid this, entrepreneurs must challenge these norms and redefine their potential.

Now that we have discussed the common mistakes to avoid when limiting beliefs and societal conditioning, let's explore the #1 piece of advice to overcome these obstacles and achieve success in entrepreneurship effectively.

My #1 Piece Of Advice

Believe in yourself and your abilities. Don't allow what people have said about you in the past, present, or future to determine your direction in life. People will always have opinions about you, but you can choose not to own those opinions. **YOU** choose who you want to be in life and then follow the steps in this chapter to bring that person to life.

Now that we have explored the various factors contributing to limiting beliefs and some strategies to overcome them, I want to share a process with you that I have used for over 25 years. Anytime I am dealing with a limiting belief, this is what I use to "kick" that limiting belief to the curb.

Please take the time to work through this as many times as you need. It will genuinely make a difference in your life.

8-Step Process For Kicking Your Limiting Beliefs To The Curb!

1. **Identify a limiting belief that is holding you back.**

    - I'm too old; I need to be a better leader; I'm not worthy of success.

2. **Ask yourself if this belief is true.**

    - Read the belief aloud and ask yourself, "Do I know this belief is true?"

3. **Determine the source of the belief.**

    - Did it stem from family beliefs? Education? Experience?

4. **Write out a Declaration Statement**

    - Declare to yourself, "I will no longer believe or be limited by this belief anymore."

5. **See yourself being free from that belief.**

   - What would your life and business look like without that belief?
   - How would it change the things in you?
   - How would it change your life?

6. **Replace the limiting belief with a new empowering belief.**

   - If you have a belief where you think, "I am not a strong leader," then replace that with, "Every day, I am becoming a better, stronger, more confident leader.

7. **Find evidence for your new belief.**

8. **Repeat the process with any limiting belief you have.**

   - In this chapter, we explored the formation of limiting beliefs and strategies to overcome them. To truly conquer self-doubt, entrepreneurs must understand the significance of having a clear vision and purpose, which we will delve into next. So, keep reading to discover how defining your goals and mission can powerfully propel you forward on your entrepreneurial journey!

CHAPTER 4

THE POWER OF PURPOSE: WHY HAVING A CLEAR VISION IS CRUCIAL TO OVERCOMING SELF-DOUBT.

"If you have a strong purpose in life, you don't have to be pushed. Your passion will drive you there." - Roy T. Bennett.

In this chapter, we will cover how to:

- Discover the powerful antidote to self-doubt that can propel entrepreneurs to success.
- Uncover the secrets to staying focused and motivated even during challenging times.
- Learn how a crystal-clear vision and purpose align your actions with long-term goals.
- Find out how a strong sense of purpose can bring deep meaning and fulfillment to your entrepreneurial journey.
- Hear a personal anecdote that will inspire you to overcome self-doubt and reignite your passion for success.

A clear vision and purpose are vital for entrepreneurs to overcome self-doubt. A solid vision and purpose for your business is an anchor during difficult times, helping you stay focused and motivated.

They provide direction and clarity, aligning your actions with your long-term goals. With a crystal-clear vision in mind, you know exactly where you're heading and why you're doing it.

Moreover, a well-defined purpose goes beyond just financial success. It taps into our deeper motivations and values, helping us connect with something larger than ourselves. When entrepreneurs have a strong sense of purpose, it brings meaning to their work, making the journey towards success all the more fulfilling and satisfying.

When self-doubt creeps in, referring back to your vision and purpose can reignite your motivation and remind you of why you embarked on this entrepreneurial journey in the first place. It brings focus back to the impact you want to create and the value you want to offer others.

To illustrate the importance of a clear vision and purpose in overcoming self-doubt, let me share a personal story. Many years ago, I faced a moment of intense self-doubt while working on a new business venture. I questioned whether I had what it takes to succeed and if my idea was truly valuable.

To overcome this doubt, I spent time revisiting my vision and purpose. I reminded myself of the problem I wanted to solve and the positive impact I aimed to make in people's lives. This exercise reaffirmed my belief in the business idea and reignited my passion and determination to see it through. And see it through, I did.

Now that you understand the importance of having a clear vision and purpose in overcoming self-doubt, I have created a checklist to help you establish and maintain a strong vision and purpose for your business. This checklist will be a practical tool to keep you focused and motivated throughout your entrepreneurial journey.

1. **Define your vision.**

Have you ever sat at your desk, pondering over your business, and wondering, "What am I trying to achieve here?" I know I have. During one of those moments, I realized the importance of clearly articulating what I wanted to achieve with my business.

Let me take you back to the early days of my entrepreneurial journey. I had just started my coaching business, and I was lost. I knew I wanted to help people and make money, but needed a clear sense of direction. That's when I decided to understand the problem I wanted to solve.

I started researching my target market, which was the network marketing profession. Before my coaching business, I built a successful business in the network marketing field. I began to realize that the things that affected me and slowed me down in my growth affected so many others in the profession: Doubt, Fear, and a Lack of Confidence.

With this newfound clarity, I could articulate the impact I wanted to make. I wanted to teach people many of the principles and strategies I learned along my journey that changed my life. I wanted to help people understand that they could learn how to manage their doubts instead of their doubts managing them. It started to light a fire within me.

But I didn't stop there. I knew that long-term goals were equally important. I wanted my business to be successful financially and have a lasting impact on the industry. I wanted to become a leader in helping people manage their mindsets and overcome the doubts they were dealing with.

In doing so, they would let other team members know what I was helping them with, creating a ripple effect of change.

So, armed with a clear understanding of the problem I wanted to solve, the impact I wanted to make, and my long-term goals for my business, I set out to create a brand that would captivate the hearts and minds of the people I served.

And you know what? It worked. By articulating my vision and purpose, I connected with my target audience on a deeper level. They saw my passion and conviction and wanted to be a part of the change I was creating. The business started to soar, and my coaching business began to thrive.

So, my fellow entrepreneurs, I urge you to articulate what you want to achieve with your business. Feel free to dig deep, understand the problem you want to solve, and envision the impact you want to make. And most importantly, always keep sight of your long-term goals. When you have a clear vision, success is just around the corner. So go out there, confidently articulate your aspirations, and realize your dreams.

2. **Identify your purpose:**

As an entrepreneur, I've learned that reflecting on the deeper motivations and values that drive me is crucial. Knowing my purpose and what truly inspires and fuels me has been a game-changer in finding meaning and success in my business.

One value that has always been at the core of my entrepreneurial journey is positively impacting others.

Nothing compares to knowing that the challenges and adversities you've gone through are now the springboard for helping others change lives. It truly is one of the greatest feelings in the world.

Another value that genuinely resonates with me is the belief in empowering others. I always taught the leaders in my business you can either enable people or empower them. When you enable them, you take away their power. They start to believe that they can't do anything on their own, which can turn into an almost "co-dependent" relationship. But when you empower people, you give them the confidence they can do it, and often, that's all they need to get the job done.

Reflecting on these deeper motivations and values has brought clarity to my entrepreneurial pursuits and immense meaning to my work. It has allowed me to build businesses that align with my core beliefs and passions, making the journey all the more fulfilling.

When you tap into your deeper motivations and values, you'll find that your business becomes more than just a means of making money; it becomes a vehicle for creating positive change, pushing boundaries, and empowering others. Embrace these values and let them guide you on your entrepreneurial journey. Trust me, the rewards and fulfillment that come with it are truly unparalleled.

3. **Write it down:**

Entrepreneurship can be an exhilarating rollercoaster ride, but it's not without its fair share of self-doubt and moments of uncertainty. That's where having a clearly defined vision and purpose, documented in writing, becomes your guiding light, your anchor in stormy seas.

Many times on my journey, I had moments of self-doubt. The challenges seemed impossible, and I began questioning whether I was on the right path. In that moment of darkness, I turned to my written vision and purpose. I opened the document and reconnected with the essence of why I started my business in the first place.

Reading those words transported me back to the initial exhilaration, the burning desire to make a difference, and the unwavering belief in my idea. It reminded me of my long-term goals and the impact I sought to create. Suddenly, all that self-doubt melted away, and I re-energized and refocused on my vision.

Having your vision and purpose in writing is like having a secret weapon against self-doubt. When you feel lost or overwhelmed, you can always return to that document and remind yourself of your greater purpose. It reignites the fire within you and renews your determination to keep pushing forward.

But it's not just about conquering self-doubt. A written vision and purpose also help you stay laser-focused on your goals. It's like a roadmap that keeps you on track, even when distractions and shiny new opportunities tempt you.

I recall a time when a tempting business opportunity presented itself. It could be a quick win but didn't align with my vision and purpose. Because I had my vision documented, I could resist the allure and stay true to my long-term goals. I knew deviating from my path would only dilute my focus and hinder my chances of achieving the impact I sought to create.

Documenting your vision and purpose is more than just an exercise in idealism. It's a practical tool that helps you navigate the often turbulent waters of entrepreneurship. It keeps you grounded, provides clarity when things get foggy, and empowers you to make decisions aligned with your more significant goals.

So, grab that pen, open that blank document, and let your vision and purpose pour onto the page. Embrace the power of writing it down and refer back to it whenever self-doubt creeps in, or distractions attempt to sidetrack you. I guarantee you'll find strength, focus, and renewed determination to create the entrepreneurial success you've always dreamt of.

4. **Review regularly:**

Let me share the story of Steve, an entrepreneur who changed the lives of thousands by putting periodic reviews of his vision and purpose into action. Like many aspiring entrepreneurs, Steve had a burning desire to make a difference. He founded a nonprofit organization that provided education and resources to underprivileged children.

However, as the years went by and the organization's demands increased, Steve found himself losing sight of his original purpose. The day-to-day operations, fundraising efforts, and administrative tasks started overshadowing the very reason he started the organization in the first place.

Determined to reconnect with his passion and remind himself of the impact he aimed to create, Steve decided to set aside time every quarter to review his vision and purpose. During these review sessions, he dove deep into the stories of the children his organization had helped. He read handwritten letters and watched videos of them expressing their gratitude for the opportunities they had received.

Through these powerful reminders, Steve reignited his passion and was able to fine-tune his goals. He realized that his organization's impact could extend beyond education. By partnering with local businesses and community leaders, he could create mentorship programs and provide career guidance to help these children break free from the cycles of poverty.

Steve transformed his organization into a powerful force for change thanks to his commitment to reviewing his vision and purpose. By staying connected to his beliefs and refining his goals, he empowered countless children to dream bigger and achieve their aspirations. Remember, whether you're running a bakery or a nonprofit, periodic reviews are essential to reaffirm your belief, reignite your passion, and refine your goals.

5. **Seek support:**

Surrounding yourself with a supportive network of mentors, coaches, or fellow entrepreneurs is like having your own cheerleading squad. When I started my journey as an entrepreneur, I had a mentor who had been through it all. Whenever I felt overwhelmed, I would ask him for guidance and advice. He not only provided me with valuable insights, but he also believed in me even when I doubted myself. I can't emphasize enough how important it is to have someone in your corner who sees your potential and pushes you to reach for the stars. So, go out there, build your support network, and watch yourself soar to new heights.

6. **Take action:**

Having a purpose and a vision is great, but more is needed. It would be best to have a clear plan and actionable steps to turn that vision into a reality.

One way to do that is to break down your big goal into smaller, achievable ones. Set a timeline for each goal and diligently work towards them. By breaking it down and taking action, you will steadily build momentum and gain the confidence to keep moving forward.

7. **Celebrate milestones:**

I have several friends who love to run marathons. One of my friends runs the New York Marathon every year. 26.2 miles of running! I run from my house to my mailbox and back to my house, and I'm ready to pass out. I can't even imagine 26 miles.

Over 50,000 people every year participate in the marathon. Along the course, they have mile markers posted at every mile. Why do they do that? It's simply to celebrate each little victory on the road to the big success, finishing the race.

Can you imagine running that long, not knowing how far you've gone or how far you have left to go? It could get discouraging after a while. But you can celebrate being one mile closer to completing the marathon every mile you finish.

It's the same principle in business. Don't wait to accomplish your big, end-of-the-month goal to celebrate. Celebrate the little victories along the way. Celebrate the progress you are making. When you do that, you encourage yourself to keep moving forward, pushing your doubts aside. Make it a habit to celebrate the victories and milestones and watch what it will do to your confidence.

8. **<u>Stay resilient:</u>**

Tough times don't last; tough people do. When things don't go your way, and you feel like giving up, Stay Resilient! Remind yourself of your vision and purpose and use it as fuel to overcome obstacles and continue moving forward.

I remember a time in my business when the bottom fell out from underneath me about four years into it. My business and income dropped nearly 80%. I had just got married, bought a new house, put my son in a private high school, and now this? I was devastated. I had many sleepless nights wondering what I was going to do. How would I survive, pay the bills, and get beyond this? One thing I knew for sure: Giving up wouldn't help. So, I had to decide to be resilient: to develop the mental toughness I needed to get through it. Was it easy? Absolutely not! But with perseverance, dedication, and hard work, I was able to dig my way out of that hole and gain back all that I lost and more.

Markets change, circumstances evolve, and you must stay flexible and adjust your goals accordingly. By doing so, you'll be able to navigate challenges, seize new opportunities, and ultimately achieve your desired success.

9. **<u>Adapt and pivot:</u>**

As you progress on your entrepreneurial journey, be open to adapting and shifting your vision and purpose if needed. Markets change, circumstances evolve, and you must stay flexible and adjust your goals accordingly.

In 2020, I was excited to have my entire calendar booked for the year with speaking engagements. And then Covid hit! Instantly, my events for the whole year were canceled. I started to feel anxious as I thought, "What will I do? How am I going to make money? Take care of my family?" It was a scary time.

I knew that to survive, I would have to adjust and pivot. I decided to learn how to do virtual events. Technology to me is like having a root canal with no Novocain: Painful! But I began researching and knowing what I needed to learn to make that happen.

What was the outcome of that pivot? 2020 became the most significant growth year in my business history. I could do all my events without leaving my home office.

All that happened because I embraced the challenge, pivoted, and created a solution that made sense. I could still make a difference in people's lives, more so than any previous year. It was a great learning experience for me.

10. **Continuously reflect and refine:**

Recently, I had the opportunity to interview a good friend who has built a thriving wellness business. When I asked her about the secret to her success, she shared a personal anecdote that resonated with me.

She started her business with a clear vision and purpose: to help people live healthier and happier lives.

However, as her business grew, she got caught up in the day-to-day operations and lost sight of her original vision. Only when she took a step back and regularly reflected on her progress did she realize she needed to reevaluate her vision and purpose.

By revisiting her long-term goals and reconnecting with her passion, she was able to steer her business in a new direction. She developed new products and services aligned with her original vision, which paid off. Her brand experienced a rejuvenation, and her customers responded positively to the changes.

Regularly reflecting on your progress and reevaluating your vision and purpose is crucial for long-term success. It allows you to realign your goals and ensure that you constantly grow and evolve in the right direction.

Following these steps, you can leverage your clear vision and purpose to overcome self-doubt and build a successful and impactful business.

My #1 Piece Of Advice

Clarify your values, passions, and long-term objectives to align your business with your purpose, creating a solid foundation for overcoming doubt and fear.

As we have seen, having a clear vision and purpose is crucial for entrepreneurs to overcome self-doubt, but what happens when our vison and purpose gets criticized or receives negative feedback? Don't worry, we are going to go through some great steps in the next chapter on how to deal with that. So, turn the page and let's keep on growing.

CHAPTER 5

THICK SKIN, STRONG SPIRIT: NAVIGATING CRITICISM AND NEGATIVE FEEDBACK

"The only way to avoid criticism is to do nothing, say nothing, and be nothing." - Aristotle.

In this chapter, we will cover how to:

- Discover how entrepreneurs can transform criticism into constructive feedback and propel personal and professional growth.

- Learn how to filter out irrelevant criticism and maintain confidence in your abilities as an entrepreneur.

- Explore the importance of building a solid support network and gathering diverse perspectives to validate your ideas and strategies.

- Find out how relying on data and objective evidence can strengthen your defense against negative feedback and boost your confidence.

- Uncover the secrets to developing resilience and coping mechanisms to navigate criticism and maintain your emotional well-being in the entrepreneurial journey.

As entrepreneurs, you will face criticism and negative feedback regularly, which can be daunting and potentially detrimental to your confidence. However, by adopting specific strategies and approaches, you can effectively deal with criticism and negative feedback while maintaining self-confidence.

First, you must view criticism as an opportunity for improvement rather than a personal attack. Embracing criticism as a means of growth allows you to detach from negative feedback and approach it objectively and emotionally. By cultivating a mindset focused on continuous learning and self-improvement, you can transform criticism into constructive feedback that propels your personal and professional growth.

Second, you should understand the intention behind the criticism or negative feedback. Is it coming from a knowledgeable and experienced source or solely based on personal opinion? Valid criticism, coming from individuals with expertise in the relevant field, can provide valuable insights and help you identify areas for improvement. On the other hand, you should discard criticism driven by personal biases or without constructive intent. By discerning the purpose behind the feedback, you can filter out irrelevant or unfounded criticism and maintain your confidence in your abilities.

Third, actively seek feedback from diverse sources and establish a support network. You can gather different perspectives and validate their ideas and strategies. Constructive feedback from trusted individuals can counter negative feedback, ensuring that you maintain confidence in their abilities while addressing areas for growth. Building a solid support network also provides emotional support during challenging times, helping you navigate criticism without losing enthusiasm.

Fourth, you can minimize the impact of criticism by focusing on data and objective evidence. By relying on quantifiable metrics and concrete results, you can defend your decisions and actions with factual evidence. Presenting a logical and well-researched defense against negative feedback reinforces your confidence in their expertise and gives you a solid foundation to tackle criticism.

Finally, you must cultivate resilience and develop coping mechanisms for criticism. Criticism can be emotionally draining and may lead to self-doubt if mismanaged.

Dealing with criticism and negative feedback is integral to the entrepreneurial journey. The strategies I will share in this chapter can help you overcome doubt and fear, ultimately allowing you to thrive and succeed in your endeavors.

Let me share a story with you that makes me laugh every time I think about it, even though it happened almost three decades ago.

In 1995, I embarked on an extraordinary journey as I started my own network marketing business. It was a path I had never ventured upon before, and as I stood on the precipice of this new endeavor, I found myself enveloped in nervousness, fear, and doubt. The uncertainty of this venture was daunting, but little did I know even more significant challenges awaited.

To make matters worse, criticism poured in from all directions. Friends, co-workers, and even my parents joined the chorus of doubters. Their comments stung as they discredited my abilities, questioning my business knowledge and reminding me of my tendency to abandon ventures prematurely. A cloud of skepticism loomed over me, but instead of allowing it to overshadow my dreams, it fueled a fire within me.

Driven by a fierce determination, I sought to silence the voices of doubt that plagued my journey. I channeled their negativity into motivation, using their judgment and criticism as a catalyst for growth. Each doubt cast upon me became another reason to strive for success, to show them that I was more capable than their limited perceptions allowed them to believe.

And prove them wrong, I did. With relentless dedication, I rose through the ranks of my company. From the humble beginnings of a novice entrepreneur, I emerged as a Vice President leading a team towards greatness. But it didn't stop there; I opened an office in my local area, a testament to the power of perseverance in the face of adversity. Along this journey of determination, accolades became the milestones that adorned my path, a testament to my unwavering resolve.

The pinnacle of this triumph came with my office's grand opening. In a move infused with confidence and audacity, I invited all those who had criticized and doubted me. Their jaws dropped in awe as they entered my beautifully adorned 2,500 sq ft office. One particular friend, who had once dismissed my ambitions, whispered to me, "I never doubted you." Suppressing the urge to laugh, I smiled and cherished the sweet taste of success. For me, success became the ultimate form of revenge.

This story is a testament to the power of tuning out the clamor of judgment and criticism. It teaches us to rise above the noise and relentlessly pursue our dreams. Nothing builds confidence quite like triumphing over adversity. As doubts are silenced, and victories accumulate, we find strength and clarity that transcends any negativity the world might throw at us.

In life, succumbing to the shackles of doubt and criticism is easy. However, by turning a deaf ear to the naysayers and embracing our passion, we unlock the potential within us to achieve greatness. The journey may be arduous, but the rewards are indescribable. So, believe in yourself, defy the cynics, and embark on your path to victory. Remember, nothing silences doubts and builds confidence like the sweet taste of success.

How can you see judgment and criticism play out in life? Let's look at a few examples:

Examples

An entrepreneur receives feedback from a customer that their product is too expensive compared to competitors. Instead of taking it personally, the entrepreneur views this criticism as an opportunity to evaluate their pricing strategy and adjust better to meet market demands.

During a pitch presentation, an investor raises concerns about the scalability of the entrepreneur's business model. Rather than becoming discouraged, the entrepreneur appreciates this feedback as a chance to reassess and find solutions to potential scalability challenges.

A negative online review criticizes the entrepreneur's customer service. Instead of feeling demoralized, the entrepreneur proactively reaches out to the dissatisfied customer, acknowledging their concerns and offering a solution. This customer interaction resolves the issue and demonstrates the entrepreneur's commitment to excellent customer service.

As an entrepreneur seeks funding, they receive rejection after rejection from investors. Instead of losing confidence, the entrepreneur seeks input from experienced mentors and experts, fine-tuning their pitch and business model, ultimately attracting investors who appreciate their perseverance and improvements.

The founder of a startup faces criticism from their team regarding their leadership style. Rather than reacting defensively, the entrepreneur takes the feedback seriously, engages in open and honest conversations with their team, and implements changes to create a healthier and more productive work environment.

A competitor criticizes an entrepreneur's marketing campaign, claiming it lacks creativity and originality. Instead of being discouraged, the entrepreneur seeks input from their target market, gathering honest opinions and making adjustments that resonate better with their audience.

After facing a setback, such as a failed product launch, an entrepreneur reflects on the lessons learned, identifies their strengths, and develops a plan to overcome the obstacles. By embracing the experience as a learning opportunity rather than dwelling on the failure, the entrepreneur maintains their confidence and motivation to move forward.

Now that we have seen several examples of entrepreneurs embracing feedback and criticism as opportunities for growth and improvement, let's dive into a case study that highlights how one entrepreneur utilized input to enhance their business strategy and achieve success.

Case Study

Company: XYZ Tech Solutions

Background:

XYZ Tech Solutions is a startup company that provides innovative technology solutions to businesses. The company was founded by Mark Johnson, a visionary entrepreneur passionate about developing cutting-edge products. As the company grew, Mark faced various challenges and encountered criticism and negative feedback from stakeholders, which initially affected his confidence. However, he implemented strategies to develop thick skin and effectively deal with criticism, leading to significant personal and professional growth.

Key strategies and approaches implemented:

1. Adopting a growth mindset:

Mark recognized the importance of viewing criticism as an opportunity for improvement rather than a personal attack. He embraced a growth mindset, understanding that feedback, even if negative, could propel his growth. By shifting his perspective, Mark could emotionally detach himself from negative feedback and approach it objectively. He saw criticism as a valuable tool for refining his skills and adjusting his business strategies.

2. **Understanding the intention behind the feedback:**

Mark realized the importance of discerning the intent behind the criticism or negative feedback. He sought input from knowledgeable and experienced sources, such as industry experts and mentors, to gather valuable insights and identify areas for improvement. Conversely, he learned to discard irrelevant or unfounded criticism driven by personal biases or without constructive intent. This selective approach allowed Mark to maintain his confidence in his abilities while benefiting from valuable feedback.

3. **Seeking diverse feedback and establishing a support network:**

Mark actively sought feedback from diverse sources to validate his ideas and strategies. He surrounded himself with mentors, industry experts, and fellow entrepreneurs who provided different perspectives and constructive feedback. This support network helped Mark address areas for growth and provided emotional support during challenging times. By engaging with trusted individuals, Mark maintained his confidence while benefiting from constructive criticism.

4. **Relying on data and objective evidence:**

To minimize the impact of criticism, Mark focused on presenting quantifiable metrics and concrete results. He meticulously gathered data to support his decisions and actions, which allowed him to defend his strategies with factual evidence. This practice reinforced Mark's confidence in his expertise and gave him a solid foundation to tackle criticism.

By relying on tangible evidence, Mark could engage in productive discussions and address negative feedback more effectively.

Measurable outcomes achieved:

1. **Improved product quality:** By embracing criticism as an opportunity for improvement, the company enhanced the quality of its products. Valuable feedback from experts allowed Mark to identify and address weaknesses, resulting in more robust and innovative solutions.

2. **Enhanced decision-making:** Seeking diverse feedback and establishing a support network enabled Mark to make more informed decisions. The variety of perspectives and insights he gathered contributed to well-rounded strategies and improved outcomes.

3. **Increased confidence and resilience:** Through adopting a growth mindset and cultivating resilience, Mark developed thick skin and learned to bounce back from criticism. He became more confident in his abilities, positively impacting his leadership and the company's overall performance.

Challenges faced:

Despite the positive outcomes, Mark encountered several challenges along the way:

1. **Overcoming initial self-doubt:** Negative feedback and criticism took a toll on Mark's confidence. Overcoming self-doubt required time and effort but adopting strategies such as self-reflection and celebrating achievements helped him regain confidence.

2. **Navigating conflicting feedback:** Receiving feedback from diverse sources sometimes leads to contradictory opinions. Mark had to carefully assess and synthesize the feedback to determine the most appropriate course of action.

Lessons learned:

1. **Criticism as an opportunity:** Viewing criticism as a means for growth and improvement proved invaluable. Embracing feedback as an opportunity rather than a personal attack allowed them to make the necessary adjustments for success.

2. **The importance of a support network:** Developing a solid support network was crucial for maintaining confidence and navigating criticism. Having trusted individuals to provide guidance and emotional support proved invaluable in their entrepreneurial journey.

Overall assessment:

The impact of implementing strategies to develop thick skin regarding criticism and negative feedback was highly positive for XYZ Tech Solutions. Mark and his company were able to deal with criticism while maintaining confidence effectively. The strategies enabled them to thrive, resulting in improved product quality, enhanced decision-making, increased confidence, and resilience. XYZ Tech Solutions transformed criticism into constructive feedback, propelling their personal and professional growth.

Now that we have discussed the case study of XYZ Tech Solutions and how they successfully developed thick skin in the face of criticism and negative feedback let's explore some of the mistakes to avoid when dealing with criticism based on their experiences.

Typical Mistakes And How To Avoid Them

1. **Taking criticism personally**: You must develop a growth mindset and stop viewing criticism as a personal attack. Instead, embrace it as an opportunity for improvement.

2. **Ignoring the intention behind the feedback**: You should take the time to understand the source and intent behind the criticism. Valid criticism from knowledgeable individuals can be helpful, while you should disregard unfounded criticism or personal biases

3. **Seeking feedback from only one source**: You should seek feedback from diverse sources, such as mentors, industry experts, and other entrepreneurs. This allows you to gather different perspectives and validate their ideas.

4. **Not relying on objective evidence**: By basing their decisions on quantifiable metrics and concrete results, you can defend yourself against negative feedback with factual evidence. This reinforces your confidence and provides a solid foundation to tackle criticism.

5. **Neglecting self-care:** Dealing with criticism can be emotionally draining. You should practice self-reflection, develop a positive mindset, and engage in self-care activities to maintain your emotional well-being and resilience.

By adopting these strategies, you can effectively deal with criticism while maintaining your confidence and ultimately thriving in your endeavors.

Now that we have discussed the most common mistakes to avoid when dealing with criticism and negative feedback let's delve into the number one piece of advice that encompasses all of these strategies.

My #1 Piece Of Advice

Embrace criticism and negative feedback as opportunities for growth and improvement rather than taking them personally or dwelling on them.

As you learn to navigate criticism and negative feedback, it becomes crucial for you to tackle the fear of judgment or rejection that can hinder your progress. In the next chapter, let's explore strategies to overcome these challenges and gain the necessary support for your ideas. Keep reading to discover how to confidently share your vision and seek the backing you need to succeed.

CHAPTER 6

FEARLESS AND FIERCE: OVERCOMING THE FEAR OF JUDGEMENT AND REJECTION

"When others judge or reject you, it's a reflection of their limitations and insecurities. Stay true to yourself, believe in your abilities, and let their opinions fuel your determination to prove them wrong."

In this chapter, we will cover how to:

- Discover the power of Vulnerability and how it can strengthen your entrepreneurial journey.
- Learn how to turn failures into valuable learning opportunities and overcome the fear of judgment and rejection.
- Find out how thorough preparation can boost your confidence and help you defend your ideas with knowledge and facts.
- Take small steps towards overcoming your fear by gradually exposing yourself to risk and challenge. Embrace these strategies and watch your confidence soar as you conquer the fear of judgment and rejection.

Entrepreneurs often fear judgment and rejection when sharing their ideas and seeking support. However, overcoming this fear is crucial for your growth and success.

There are several strategies and techniques that you can use to build confidence and navigate through these challenges.

1. **Embrace Vulnerability**: Vulnerability is not a weakness but a strength. Sharing ideas and seeking support requires a certain level of Vulnerability, but it also opens opportunities for growth and learning. By accepting and embracing Vulnerability, you can gain confidence in your ideas and reduce the fear of judgment or rejection.

2. **Prepare thoroughly**: Confidence comes from being well-prepared. You should research and understand your ideas before sharing them with others. You can confidently present your thoughts and defend your position by having a solid understanding of your ideas and supporting evidence. This preparation helps reduce the fear of judgment and rejection, as you are armed with knowledge and facts to back your ideas.

3. **Gradual exposure to risk and challenge**: Overcoming fear requires gradual exposure to the source of fear. Encourage yourself to start by sharing your ideas with trusted individuals or in a controlled environment, gradually increasing the exposure to a broader audience. This incremental approach allows you to build confidence and develop resilience to judgment and rejection.

I have crafted a few examples to illustrate how entrepreneurs can overcome their fear of judgment and rejection. By implementing these strategies, you can build confidence in your ideas and ensure they do not hinder your progress.

<u>Examples</u>

Embrace Vulnerability: A group of entrepreneurs has created a unique idea for a new mobile app. However, they hesitate to share their vision due to fear of judgment and rejection. Despite their fear, they decide to leap of faith and pitch their idea to potential investors. By embracing Vulnerability and putting themselves out there, the entrepreneur receives valuable feedback and support, ultimately leading to their app's success.

Prepare thoroughly: A successful entrepreneur is developing a business plan for their next venture. They know they must present their idea to potential investors, so they spend weeks conducting market research, analyzing financial projections, and refining their pitch. By being well-prepared and profoundly understanding their concept, the entrepreneur gains confidence in their presentation. Their comprehensive preparation helps them overcome the fear of judgment and rejection, as they can confidently back their ideas with knowledge and evidence.

Gradual exposure to risk and challenge: A first-time entrepreneur has a brilliant idea for a product but hesitates to share it with others due to fear of negative feedback. To overcome their fear, they first share their idea with a trusted friend and ask for honest feedback. Encouraged by the positive response, they presented their concept to a small group of industry professionals. As they gradually expose themselves to risk and challenge, the entrepreneur gains confidence in their vision and becomes more comfortable sharing it with a broader audience, eventually overcoming their fear of judgment and rejection.

Now that we have explored various examples of overcoming the fear of judgment and rejection in an entrepreneurial context let's dive into a case study that illustrates the transformative power of the strategies we've shared.

Case Study

Company: ABC Tech Solutions

Background:

ABC Tech Solutions is a startup specializing in developing innovative software solutions for small businesses. The company's founder, Sam, had a brilliant idea for a new software product but was struggling with fear of judgment and rejection when sharing his vision with others and seeking support. Sam understood that overcoming this fear was crucial for the growth and success of his company, so he decided to implement strategies to move beyond judgment and rejection.

Actions/Initiatives Implemented:

1. Embracing Vulnerability.

Sam attended several entrepreneurship workshops and networking events to gain insight and guidance on navigating the business world. At one of these workshops, he had an eye-opening realization: Vulnerability is not a weakness but a strength.

One of the speakers, a successful entrepreneur, shared their journey and how being vulnerable had helped them grow personally and professionally. They stressed that they gained valuable feedback and support by opening up and sharing their ideas with trusted peers and mentors.

Inspired by this new perspective, Sam took a leap of faith and started sharing his ideas with his trusted peers and mentors. Initially, fearing judgment or rejection was nerve-wracking for him. However, he quickly discovered that his Vulnerability was met with respect and encouragement.

As he continued sharing his ideas and receiving feedback, something incredible happened - Sam's confidence grew. He became more comfortable with being vulnerable, realizing it was a powerful personal and professional growth tool. The fear of judgment or rejection started to diminish, and he could focus more on the value of his ideas.

With newfound confidence, Sam started actively seeking opportunities to share his ideas. He participated in pitch competitions and joined forums where entrepreneurs could provide feedback on each other's ideas. The more he shared, the more he learned from others, and the stronger his ideas became.

Over time, Sam's willingness to be vulnerable became one of his greatest assets. Rather than seeing Vulnerability as a weakness, he now saw it as a way to build solid connections and gain valuable insights. His network of trusted peers and mentors became an invaluable resource, supporting him throughout his entrepreneurial journey.

If you find yourself hesitating to share your ideas, remember Sam's story. Embrace Vulnerability, for it is not a weakness but a strength. By sharing your thoughts with trusted peers and mentors, you can gain confidence and reduce the fear of judgment or rejection.

Trust in the power of Vulnerability, and watch it propel your ideas to new heights.

2. **Thorough Preparation**:

Let me share a significant anecdote that perfectly illustrates the value of Sam's thorough preparation.

Sam had a brilliant idea for a new tech product. But instead of rushing to share his vision with the world, he decided to take a step back and do his due diligence.

He spent hours diving deep into market research, studying the industry landscape, and identifying potential competitors. He wanted to understand what already existed in the market and how he could differentiate his product. Armed with this knowledge, he was able to position his idea in a unique way, which ultimately became his competitive advantage.

But Sam didn't stop there. He knew that the success of his product would ultimately rely on its relevance to the users. By conducting user surveys, gathering feedback from various potential customers, genuinely listening to their needs, and incorporating their suggestions, he was able to refine his idea and make it even more appealing to his target audience.

When the time finally came to share his ideas with others, Sam was well-prepared and confident. He had anticipated potential objections, doubts, and questions and was armed with data-backed responses. This level of preparation strengthened his self-assurance and alleviated the fear of judgment and rejection that often plagues entrepreneurs.

During his presentations, Sam didn't just showcase his idea; he passionately defended it. His thorough research and preparation made it clear to everyone in the room that he had done his homework and was deeply knowledgeable about the subject matter. This instilled confidence in his audience, and they couldn't help but be captivated by his enthusiasm and expertise.

When the Q&A session rolled around, Sam was ready to address any doubts or concerns. His preparation allowed him to respond effectively and reassure even the most skeptical individuals. This solidified his credibility and convinced others to believe in his vision.

In the end, Sam's thorough preparation paid off. Thanks to his confident and well-researched presentations, he could garner support for his idea and attract potential investors and partners. His diligence and attention to detail set him apart from the crowd and gave his thoughts the strong foundation they needed to succeed.

So, the next time you have a great idea or an important presentation, take a page from Sam's book. Invest the time to research and understand your concept thoroughly. Gather data, analyze the market, and seek feedback from potential users. By doing so, you can confidently present your thoughts, defend your position, and ultimately succeed in turning your ideas into reality.

3. Gradual Exposure to Risk and Challenge:

Sam had always been full of innovative ideas but struggled with a crippling fear of judgment and rejection. So, he decided to take small steps to overcome his fear gradually.

At first, he started by sharing his ideas with a close circle of trusted friends and family members. He knew they would provide a safe and supportive environment for him to express his thoughts without fear of harsh criticism. By receiving positive feedback and encouragement from his loved ones, Sam's confidence began to grow.

Buoyed by his newfound courage, Sam took the next step and presented his ideas in local startup pitch competitions and entrepreneurship events. It was a giant leap for him, but he believed that exposing himself to a broader audience would help him build even more confidence.

The first few events were nerve-wracking for him. He had to take deep breaths and remind himself that rejection was a part of the process. But Sam gradually became more comfortable putting himself out there with each presentation. He learned to embrace the feedback, whether positive or negative, as an opportunity for growth and improvement.

As he continued this incremental path, something unique happened. People in the startup community started to take notice of his ideas. They admired his tenacity and determination to overcome his fear. Slowly but surely, Sam began to receive increased support and validation for his ideas.

Sam's confidence soared to new heights with the newfound support and validation. He no longer feared judgment or rejection because he knew he had a strong support system behind him. This resilience allowed him to take more risks and pursue even greater goals.

In the end, Sam's gradual approach paid off. His ideas gained traction, and he became known as an up-and-coming entrepreneur in his community. And it all started with that first small step of sharing his thoughts with his inner circle.

So, my friends, if you're struggling with fear and self-doubt, take inspiration from Sam's journey. Start by sharing your ideas with a close circle of trusted friends and family members. As you gain confidence, gradually expose yourself to a broader audience through events or competitions. Embrace judgment and rejection as opportunities for growth. And most importantly, always appreciate the power of building relationships and seeking support from those who believe in you.

Remember, success doesn't happen overnight. It's a journey of incremental steps, resilience, and unwavering confidence.

Measurable Outcomes Achieved:

-ABC Tech Solutions received funding from a venture capitalist after Sam pitched his idea at a startup pitch competition, showcasing his newfound confidence and overcoming the fear of judgment and rejection.

- ABC Tech Solutions experienced a significant increase in user adoption and sales after Sam implemented feedback from potential customers, allowing him to address concerns and improve the product.

- Sam successfully recruited top talent to join ABC Tech Solutions, as his confidence in presenting the company's vision and goals attracted highly skilled individuals who believed in his ideas.

Challenges Faced:

- Sam initially faced skepticism and criticism when sharing his ideas with others, which was challenging to navigate. However, with the support of his mentors and peer group, he learned to filter the feedback constructively and use it as an opportunity for improvement.

- Overcoming the fear of judgment and rejection required consistent effort and perseverance. Sam faced moments of self-doubt and uncertainty, but he learned to trust in his abilities and focus on the value of his ideas.

Overall Impact:

By implementing these strategies, Sam overcame his fear of judgment and rejection, allowing ABC Tech Solutions to thrive. The company gained funding, experienced increased user adoption, and attracted top talent. Sam's newfound confidence and resilience positively impacted the growth and success of the company. The lessons learned from this experience will continue to shape Sam's entrepreneurial journey and contribute to his future endeavors.

Now that we have examined the case study of ABC Tech Solutions and Sam's journey of overcoming the fear of judgment and rejection let's delve into a list of mistakes to avoid when facing similar challenges.

Typical Mistakes And How To Avoid Them

Based on the material covered in this chapter, most people make the mistake of letting fear hold them back from sharing their ideas and seeking support.

This fear of judgment and rejection can hinder their growth and success as entrepreneurs. However, there are ways to avoid these mistakes and overcome this fear.

One common mistake is seeing Vulnerability as a weakness. Encouraging yourself

to embrace Vulnerability and understand that it is a strength can help you gain confidence in sharing your ideas. By accepting and embracing Vulnerability, you can open up to growth and learning opportunities.

Another mistake is associating judgment and rejection with failure. This negative association can increase the fear of sharing ideas. Instead, you should reframe failure as a learning opportunity. Seeing setbacks as valuable experiences that can lead to growth and improvement can help them overcome the fear of judgment and rejection.

Being well-prepared is another critical aspect. Confidence comes from knowing one's ideas and being able to defend them. Investing time in researching and understanding your ideas before sharing them with others can help you confidently present your thoughts. This preparation reduces the fear of judgment and rejection as you are armed with knowledge and facts to back your ideas.

The last mistake is overcoming fear, which requires gradual exposure to the source of fear. Starting by sharing ideas with trusted individuals or in a controlled environment and gradually increasing the exposure to a broader audience can help build confidence over time. This approach will allow you to develop resilience to judgment and rejection.

As we begin to wrap up this chapter, let me share this thought with you;

My #1 Piece Of Advice

Embrace rejection and see it as a learning opportunity to grow and improve.

Remember that most of the time, people are not rejecting you personally; they are rejecting (sometimes temporarily) what you're offering them. Don't give up! Stay persistent because you never know when the time will be suitable for that person or company to do business with you.

Now that we have explored several strategies and techniques to help you overcome the fear of judgment and rejection, it's time to implement these principles.

I created a checklist that summarizes essential steps to build confidence and navigate these challenges. By following this checklist, you can ensure you are well-prepared and equipped to face whatever fears come your way.

Action Steps Checklist:

1. Embrace Vulnerability:

- Encourage yourself to recognize Vulnerability as a strength rather than a weakness.

- Emphasize the opportunities for growth and learning that come with sharing ideas and seeking support.

- Learn how to accept and embrace Vulnerability to reduce fear of judgment or rejection.

2. **Prepare thoroughly:**

- Understand the importance of thorough research and understanding of your ideas.

- Invest time in gathering facts and evidence to support your ideas.

- Develop a solid understanding that will enable you to present and defend your thoughts confidently.

3. **Gradual exposure to risk and challenge:**

- Start sharing your ideas with trusted individuals or in controlled environments.

- Gradually increase exposure to a broader audience over time.

- Continue this process, and your audience will grow over time.

We've covered a lot of ground, but the journey doesn't end here because as you start to overcome your fear of judgment and rejection, you often face another emotional hurdle that can hold you back—imposter syndrome and the feeling of not being "authentic" or "good enough."

The next chapter will explore practical strategies for conquering imposter syndrome and building confidence in your entrepreneurial abilities. So don't stop now! Keep reading to unlock the key to becoming your most authentic and confident self.

CHAPTER 7

UNMASKING THE IMPOSTER BEAST: THE CONNECTION BETWEEN SELF-DOUBT AND IMPOSTER SYNDROME IN ENTREPRENEURIAL LEADERSHIP

"Believe in yourself and all that you are. Know that there is something inside you that is greater than any obstacle." - Christian D. Larson.

In this chapter, we will cover how to:

- Discover the hidden connection between self-doubt and imposter syndrome that could sabotage your success.

- Uncover how imposter syndrome can hinder your leadership potential as an entrepreneur.

- Learn how imposter syndrome can erode trust and credibility in your relationships, affecting collaboration and productivity.

- Find out how imposter syndrome can create a fear of failure, hindering your ability to take essential risks for growth and innovation.

- Discover powerful strategies to overcome imposter syndrome, regain confidence, and become the inspiring leader you are meant to be.

To truly understand the connection between self-doubt and imposter syndrome, we must first recognize that imposter syndrome manifests our deepest insecurities and self-doubts. That nagging voice in our head whispers, "You're not good enough" or "You don't deserve your success."

Regarding entrepreneurs and their leadership roles, imposter syndrome can be particularly debilitating. Our ability to lead and inspire is paramount to our success. However, if we constantly doubt ourselves and feel like frauds, making confident decisions and effectively guiding our teams becomes challenging.

Imposter syndrome can hinder an entrepreneur's leadership potential in several ways. First, it leads to a lack of self-confidence. When we constantly doubt our abilities, we are less likely to take risks, voice our opinions, or make decisive moves. This can result in missed opportunities and a stagnant business.

Second, imposter syndrome erodes trust and credibility in our relationships with our team members and external stakeholders. Others may also question our abilities and leadership capabilities when we doubt ourselves. This can lead to a fractured team dynamic and ultimately hinder collaboration and productivity.

Lastly, imposter syndrome can lead to a fear of failure. As entrepreneurs, we must be willing to fail and learn from our mistakes. However, being plagued by thoughts of "I'm not good enough," we may become averse to taking risks essential for growth and innovation.

The impact of imposter syndrome on entrepreneurs in their leadership roles is immense. However, it is crucial to remember that we have the power to overcome and regain our confidence as leaders.

Acknowledging our doubts and insecurities can challenge and reframe our negative self-talk. We must recognize that it is normal to feel uncertain and embrace that growth only comes through taking risks and pushing beyond our comfort zones.

In conclusion, the connection between self-doubt and imposter syndrome is undeniable. Remember, by embracing our vulnerabilities and recognizing our true worth, we can unleash our full potential and make a lasting impact on our entrepreneurial journeys.

Let's look at a case study to understand how these principles can apply to your business.

Case Study

Background: John is an entrepreneur who has built a successful startup in the technology industry. However, he constantly feels like a fraud and doubts his leadership abilities. His self-doubt and imposter syndrome have started to hinder his decision-making abilities and strain relationships within his team.

Actions and Initiatives Implemented:

1. Acknowledging Doubts and Insecurities:

John constantly feels he doesn't deserve his accomplishments and worries that others will discover he's a fraud.

Recognizing and acknowledging his imposter syndrome was the first step for him. He realized his negative self-talk was hindering his growth and holding him back from taking risks. So, he decided to take action and seek help.

John started by attending workshops and counseling sessions focused on imposter syndrome. In these settings, he could connect with others experiencing similar feelings of self-doubt. It was a relief for him to realize he wasn't alone in this struggle. This support network became a valuable resource for John, allowing him to share his fears and learn from others who had overcome imposter syndrome.

John began to gain a deep understanding of the root causes of his self-doubt. He discovered that it stemmed from childhood experiences and unrealistic expectations he had set for himself. Armed with this knowledge, he could challenge and reframe his negative beliefs in a more positive light.

As he delved deeper into his journey of self-discovery, John noticed a transformation in his mindset. He started to replace his self-doubt with self-compassion, recognizing that everyone makes mistakes and that failure is simply a stepping stone to success. This newfound confidence allowed him to take risks and pursue opportunities that he would have previously shied away from.

One day, John found himself in a meeting with potential investors. In the past, he would have felt like an imposter in this setting, questioning his worthiness of their attention. But this time was different. John walked into the room with a newfound sense of confidence and self-assuredness.

As he presented his business plan, John spoke passionately and persuasively. He knew his ideas were valuable and had the expertise to back them up. The investors were captivated by his confidence and vision, and by the end of the meeting, they were ready to commit.

John's journey to overcome imposter syndrome wasn't easy, but it was worth it. He built the confidence and self-assuredness necessary to achieve his goals.

Take a page from John's book if you're struggling with imposter syndrome. Recognize that you're not alone, seek support, and challenge those negative thoughts. With time and effort, you can overcome imposter syndrome and unlock your full potential.

2. Building a Supportive Network:

John knows the power of surrounding himself with the right people. He actively seeks mentors and peers who have faced similar struggles in their entrepreneurial journeys. He understands that by connecting with individuals who have already trodden the path he is on, he can gain valuable insights and learn from their experiences.

John immerses himself in entrepreneurial communities and attends networking events to find mentors and peers. These communities and events are fantastic opportunities for him to meet like-minded individuals who are driven and ambitious. John can tap into a wealth of knowledge and support by building relationships with these individuals.

One powerful anecdote that speaks to the value of seeking out mentors and peers comes from John's experience at a networking event. He was introduced to a successful entrepreneur who had faced similar challenges in his industry. The mentor was kind enough to share his struggles and how he overcame them. This conversation gave John a fresh perspective on his challenges and inspired him to keep pushing forward.

Another specific idea John employs is joining online communities or forums to connect with entrepreneurs worldwide. These platforms allow him to share his struggles and seek advice from those who may have faced similar obstacles. By actively participating in these communities, he can build relationships and access a more comprehensive network of support and knowledge.

In addition to seeking out mentors and peers, John actively participates in entrepreneurial communities and events to surround himself with individuals who share his mindset. These communities and events provide a fertile ground for feedback and encouragement. John knows an environment where everyone is committed to achieving their goals can inspire and empower.

So, whether it's joining an entrepreneur-focused Facebook group, attending a local meetup, or even participating in a mastermind group, John actively seeks out opportunities to connect with like-minded individuals. Through these interactions, he continues to learn, grow, and be motivated to overcome any obstacles that come his way.

Remember, as an entrepreneur, it's not just about the destination - it's about the journey. Surrounding yourself with mentors and peers who have been through similar struggles can make that journey more worthwhile and rewarding.

So, seek out those communities, events, and individuals who will give you the feedback, encouragement, and inspiration you need to succeed.

Measurable Outcomes Achieved:

1. **Improved Confidence and Decision-making**: As John tries to overcome his imposter syndrome, he notices a significant improvement in his confidence levels. He becomes more willing to take risks, voice his opinions, and make decisive moves, leading to better decision-making for his business.

2. **Strengthened Relationships**: By sharing his struggles with his team members and seeking feedback, John builds trust and credibility within his team. The open communication and support lead to a more cohesive and productive work environment.

3. **Embracing Failure and Innovation**: As John becomes more comfortable with failure, he encourages his team to take risks and innovate. This results in greater creativity and growth opportunities for the business.

Challenges Faced:

1. **Overcoming Negative Self-talk**: John faces challenges in reframing his negative self-talk and self-doubt. Changing his mindset and replacing self-limiting beliefs with more positive and empowering thoughts takes time and consistent effort.

2. **Vulnerability and Seeking Help**: It is initially challenging for John to admit his struggles and seek help from others. Overcoming his fear of vulnerability is a significant hurdle in overcoming imposter syndrome.

Lessons Learned:

1. **Self-awareness is Key**: John can counteract self-doubt by recognizing his strengths and accomplishments. Celebrating successes, no matter how small helps cultivate self-confidence and combat imposter syndrome.

2. A **Supportive Network is Essential**: Surrounding himself with individuals who understand his struggles and can provide honest feedback and encouragement is crucial for overcoming imposter syndrome. Building a solid support system enables John to gain perspective and realize that he is not alone in his journey.

Overall Assessment of Impact:

John's journey in overcoming imposter syndrome positively impacts his entrepreneurial leadership. His transformation allows him to unleash his full potential as a leader, moving his entrepreneurial journey and his business's success.

Now that we have examined John's journey in overcoming imposter syndrome and its positive impact on his entrepreneurial leadership let's explore one more journey: Mine!

In 2011, I took a leap of faith and ventured into the world of network marketing. My business? Financial services. You might be thinking, "Wow, what a great idea! Helping people manage their finances sounds like a dream come true!" Well, hold that thought because let me paint you a little picture of my life at that time.

I was broke! Living-in-a-300-square-foot-casita broke. And not only that, but I was also $26,000 in credit card debt. It was indeed a glamorous existence, let me tell you.

Oh, and did I mention the cherry on top? I was borrowing money from my friends to put gas in my car. Yes, you read that correctly. Gas money had become a luxury item for me.

Now, picture this: There I was, with my empty wallet and my desperate need for cash, trying to convince families that I could teach them how to manage their finances and get out of debt. I felt like a complete imposter, pretending to be someone I was not. How could I possibly have the audacity to preach about responsible financial management when I couldn't even rub two pennies together? It wasn't very uncomfortable.

But you know what? I eventually realized that I did have something valuable to offer. I may not have had a bulging bank account or a shiny credit score, but I had something even more valuable - knowledge. I learned so much by starting my own business and dealing with financial struggles I had never encountered before. And I knew that this newfound wisdom could help the families I served.

It was a revelation. I had never truly appreciated the power of the information I had acquired until I started sharing it with others. Suddenly, the imposter syndrome began to dissolve, and confidence started bubbling up from within. I became less focused on what I needed and more aware of the difference I could make in people's lives. It was like finding a hidden talent, only to realize it was there all along.

So, there you have it: My journey from being a broke, penniless imposter to becoming a resourceful, knowledge-spreading financial professional. Who would have thought that the struggling me, with all my credit card debt and gas money borrowing antics, could actually make a difference? Life has a funny way of teaching us valuable lessons, even when we least expect it.

And hey, if I can overcome imposter syndrome, anyone can. Trust me, I'm a recovered, pretending professional.

Let's explore some common mistakes to avoid when facing imposter syndrome. By learning from these mistakes, entrepreneurs can navigate their journeys more effectively and ultimately unleash their full potential as leaders.

Typical Mistakes And How To Avoid Them

1. **Not acknowledging and addressing the issue:** Many people ignore or dismiss their feelings of self-doubt and imposter syndrome instead of confronting them head-on. This can prevent them from taking the necessary steps to overcome these challenges.

How to avoid it: The first step is recognizing and acknowledging that you are experiencing imposter syndrome or self-doubt. By doing so, you can then take proactive measures to address it and work towards building self-confidence.

2. **Believing negative self-talk:** Imposter syndrome can be fueled by negative self-talk, where individuals constantly doubt their abilities and feel like frauds. Believing these thoughts can be detrimental and hinder personal and professional growth.

How to avoid it: Challenge and reframe your negative self-talk. Remind yourself of your accomplishments and strengths. Focus on positive affirmations and surround yourself with people who uplift and support you.

3. **Isolating oneself**: When feeling like an imposter, it is common for individuals to isolate themselves and believe that they are the only ones experiencing these feelings. This can lead to a lack of support and hinder personal development.

How to avoid it: Build a supportive network of mentors, peers, and friends who understand your struggles. Surround yourself with people who can provide honest feedback, encouragement, and perspective. Remember that you are not alone in your journey.

4. **Fear of taking risks**: Imposter syndrome can create a fear of failure and a reluctance to take risks. This can limit opportunities for growth and innovation in both personal and professional life.

How to avoid it: Embrace failure as a natural part of the learning process. Take calculated risks and view them as opportunities for growth and improvement. Learn from your mistakes and celebrate the progress you make along the way.

5. **Focusing on perfectionism**: Imposter syndrome often stems from the pressure to be perfect. Striving for perfection can paralyze individuals and prevent them from taking action or making decisions.

How to avoid it: Embrace the concept of progress over perfection. Understand that nobody is perfect and that growth and learning come from taking imperfect actions. Set realistic goals and celebrate your achievements, no matter how small they may seem.

Now that we have identified common mistakes people make when dealing with imposter syndrome and self-doubt let's explore my #1 advice to avoid these pitfalls.

My #1 Piece Of Advice

My advice in dealing with imposter syndrome is always to be who you are. Don't try to act or be like someone you're not. Have the confidence that even though you may not have the success you want yet; you still have value and information you can share to make a difference in people's lives. Don't let fear and doubt hold you back. Adapt and keep moving forward with confidence and determination; soon, you will feel that imposter syndrome disappear.

Now that we understand the impact of imposter syndrome, it's important to have actionable steps to combat this challenge. I've created a summary that outlines the strategies and practices we discussed to overcome imposter syndrome. Review this list anytime you need to dig yourself out of that hole. It will make a big difference.

Action Steps Checklist:

1. **Acknowledge and challenge negative self-talk:** Recognize your doubts and insecurities and actively challenge them by reframing them in a more positive and realistic light. Remember that it is normal to feel uncertain and that growth come from taking risks.

4. **Take calculated risks:** Overcome your fear of failure by embracing the mindset that failure is a learning opportunity. Push yourself beyond your comfort zone and be willing to take risks essential for growth and innovation.

5. **Prioritize open and honest communication:** Build trust and credibility in your relationships by fostering open and direct

communication with your team members and external stakeholders. Create an environment where everyone feels comfortable expressing their thoughts and opinions.

6. **Set realistic goals**: Break down your larger goals into smaller, achievable milestones. Focusing on these smaller victories can build confidence and momentum toward achieving your goals.

7. **Practice self-care**: Take care of your physical and mental well-being to maintain a positive mindset and reduce stress. Make time for activities that recharge and rejuvenate you, such as exercise, meditation, or hobbies.

8. **Continuously learn and grow**: Invest in personal and professional development through ongoing learning. Seek opportunities for skills development, attend workshops or conferences, and stay informed about industry trends and best practices.

9. **Stay resilient**: Recognize that setbacks and challenges are part of the entrepreneurial journey. Develop resilience by adopting a growth mindset, learning from failures, and persevering in adversity.

10. **Celebrate your progress**: Take time to acknowledge and celebrate your achievements. Recognize that overcoming imposter syndrome is a journey; each step forward is a testament to your growth and resilience.

As we have explored the detrimental impact of self-doubt and imposter syndrome on entrepreneurs in their leadership roles, it is now crucial to delve into another pervasive issue: the link between self-doubt and procrastination.

In the following chapter, we will uncover the connection between these two and offer valuable strategies for entrepreneurs to combat this barrier, ultimately empowering them to become more productive and confident in their endeavors. Keep reading, and you'll discover practical tips to overcome this challenge and unlock your full potential as an entrepreneur.

CHAPTER 8

PROCRASTINATION TO POWER: BREAKING FREE FROM DOUBTS DEADLY GRIP ON SUCCESS

"Don't put off tomorrow what you can do today. Have the discipline to get it done." – Ilene Roisentul.

In this chapter, we will cover how to:

- Discover the powerful connection between doubt and procrastination that keeps many entrepreneurs from success.

- Learn the key steps to break free from the cycle of doubt and procrastination and transition to a state of discipline.

- Harness the power of self-awareness and mindset shift to challenge your doubts and change your narrative.

- Create a clear roadmap by setting specific goals and taking action, gradually building momentum, and overcoming doubt.

- Witness the inspiring transformations of real entrepreneurs who embraced discipline and conquered their doubts, achieving remarkable success.

The struggle of transitioning from procrastination to discipline is tangible. It's a topic that many entrepreneurs, and frankly, individuals from all walks of life, grapple with daily.

But fear not, for I am here to shed some light on this connection between doubt and procrastination and guide you toward discipline and success.

First, let's remind ourselves about "Dan Doubt." Doubt is that sneaky little voice in our heads that whispers, "You can't do it," or "What if you fail?" It creeps in when we least expect it and hinders our progress. Doubt constantly questions our abilities, making it easier for us to succumb to procrastination. When we doubt ourselves, we tend to avoid taking action, convincing ourselves that we'll never succeed anyway, so why bother trying?

Here's the link between doubt and procrastination: doubt breeds fear, and fear breeds procrastination. When we doubt ourselves, we become afraid of failure or disappointment. We fear our efforts may fail to meet our or others' expectations, leading us to delay action. Procrastination becomes a comfort zone because it prevents us from facing doubts and potential failures.

So, how do we break free from this cycle and transition to a state of discipline? It all starts with self-awareness and a mindset shift.

1. **Awareness is** critical: Recognize your doubt and its presence in your life. Only by confronting it head-on can you begin to address it.

2. **Challenge your doubts**: Question the validity of your doubts and explore the evidence to support or contradict them. Often, you'll realize that these doubts are irrational and based on unfounded fears.

3. **Change your narrative**: Reframe your self-talk and replace negative thoughts with positive affirmations. Remind yourself of past successes and the skills you possess that make you capable of achieving greatness.

4. **Set clear goals**: Break down your aspirations into specific, actionable steps. Creating a roadmap gives you a clear direction to follow, making it harder for doubt to hold you back.

5. **Take the plunge**: Start with small, manageable tasks and gradually build momentum. Action is the antidote to doubt and procrastination. The more you act, the less power doubt will hold over you.

6. **Cultivate discipline through habit-building**: Discipline is not an innate trait but a skill that can be developed through consistent practice. Establish a routine, prioritize your tasks, and hold yourself accountable.

Remember, this journey from procrastination to discipline is not a smooth ride. There will be bumps along the way, doubts, and fears that resurface occasionally. But by persevering and staying committed to your goals, you'll gradually build the discipline and resilience needed to conquer procrastination and overcome doubt.

I've witnessed remarkable transformations in individuals who have embraced discipline and conquered their doubts. One such entrepreneur I worked with had always doubted her ability to launch a business. However, by implementing these strategies and relentlessly pursuing her goals, she successfully launched her venture and secured funding from investors captivated by her unwavering determination.

So, my friends, take this inspiration and run with it. Embrace discipline, let go of doubt, and watch the magic unfold. The road may be challenging, but the rewards are worth the effort. Procrastination will be a thing of the past, and discipline will become your steadfast companion, propelling you toward the success you deserve.

Now that we've explored the connection between doubt and procrastination and discussed some strategies for overcoming them, it's time to implement these insights.

Let's look at some examples that illustrate how to put these steps into practice and overcome doubt and procrastination.

<u>**Examples**</u>

John is a student who constantly doubts his intelligence and ability to succeed in his classes. He becomes overwhelmed with fear of failure whenever he has a big assignment or exam. As a result, he procrastinates and avoids studying, convincing himself that he's not intelligent enough to do well. By recognizing his doubts, challenging their validity, and reframing his self-talk, John builds the discipline to study consistently and effectively.

Sarah is an aspiring writer who has always dreamed of publishing a novel. However, she doubts her writing skills and fears rejection from publishers. This fear of failure leads her to procrastinate on writing and submitting her work. Through self-awareness and a change in mindset, Sarah confronts her doubts and realizes she's been holding herself back. S he begins setting clear goals, breaking down her writing process into manageable steps, and challenging her doubts by taking action. As a result, Sarah finishes her novel and successfully publishes it, overcoming her procrastination and doubt.

Mike wants to start his own business but constantly doubts his ability to succeed. He worries about the risks involved and fears that he doesn't have the necessary skills or resources. This doubt leads him to procrastinate taking the steps needed to launch his business. However, by challenging his doubts and reframing his self-talk, Mike begins to believe in himself and his abilities. He sets clear goals, creates a detailed business plan, and starts taking small actions each day. Over time, Mike builds the discipline necessary to navigate the challenges of entrepreneurship, overcoming his doubts and procrastination.

Emily is a professional athlete who is constantly plagued by doubt. She worries that she needs to be stronger and more talented to compete against top athletes in her field. This doubt causes her to procrastinate on training and miss out on opportunities for improvement. Through self-awareness and a mindset shift, Emily confronts her doubt and realizes that she has achieved success in the past due to her hard work and dedication. She sets clear goals, establishes a rigorous training routine, and pushes through her doubts by consistently taking action. As a result, Emily becomes a top competitor in her sport, overcoming her procrastination and doubt.

David is an employee who doubts his ability to excel in his job. He constantly questions whether he has the skills and knowledge necessary to succeed. This doubt causes him to procrastinate on important tasks and hold himself back from taking on new challenges. However, David begins to build confidence in his abilities by challenging his doubts and focusing on his past successes and strengths. He sets clear goals, develops a plan to enhance his skills, and consistently takes action to improve. Through discipline and perseverance, David breaks free from his procrastination and doubt, achieving success and recognition in his career.

Now that we have explored several examples of individuals overcoming doubt and procrastination let's delve into a detailed case study that illustrates the transformative power of challenging self-doubt.

Case Study

Company: XYZ Consulting

Background:

XYZ Consulting is a small consulting firm specializing in providing strategic solutions to businesses in the technology sector. The company has been in operation for five years and has faced challenges related to procrastination and lack of discipline among its team members. The founder, Stephanie, recognized the negative impact of procrastination on productivity and sought to address it within the organization.

Objectives:

The key objective of the initiative was to shift from a culture of procrastination to one of discipline, ultimately improving productivity and achieving business goals.

Outlined below are the specific actions and initiatives implemented to achieve this objective.

Actions and Initiatives:

1. **Awareness and Mindset Shift:**

- Stephanie conducted a company-wide workshop to raise awareness about the connection between doubt, procrastination, and lack of discipline.

- Employees were encouraged to self-reflect and identify instances where doubt hindered their progress.

- The workshop focused on changing the narrative and promoting positive self-talk to overcome doubts.

2. **Challenging Doubts:**

- Employees were encouraged to question the validity of their doubts and examine evidence supporting or contradicting them.

- Stephanie introduced weekly reflection sessions where team members shared their doubts and received feedback and support from colleagues.

3. **Goal Setting:**

- Clear goals were established for each department and team member, breaking them into specific, actionable steps.

- To track progress, address challenges, and adjust goals, Stephanie conducted a regular goal review meeting

4. Taking action:

- Employees were encouraged to start with small, manageable tasks to build momentum and gain confidence.

- Accountability partners were assigned to each team member to support and hold them accountable for taking action.

5. Habit-Building and Discipline:

- Stephanie encouraged the development of discipline through consistent practice.

- She implemented a rewards system to incentivize and recognize disciplined behavior

- Employees were advised to establish daily routines, prioritize tasks, and focus on their goals.

Measurable Outcomes:

1. **Improved Productivity**: The company saw a 20% increase in overall productivity within the first six months of implementing the initiatives. Employees reported feeling more focused and motivated to complete tasks.

2. **Goal Achievement**: By setting clear goals and taking consistent action, the company witnessed a 30% increase in goal achievement rates. Employees felt a sense of accomplishment and satisfaction as they reached their targets.

Challenges Faced:

1. **Resistance to Change**: Some team members initially resisted the shift from procrastination to discipline, finding it difficult to break

old habits. Regular reminders and coaching sessions were conducted to address resistance and provide support.

2. **Sustaining Discipline**: Maintaining discipline over the long term proved challenging for some employees. Continued reinforcement and periodic workshops were necessary to reinforce the importance of discipline and address any lapses.

Lessons Learned:

1. **Self-awareness is crucial**: Recognizing doubts and their impact on procrastination is the first step towards overcoming them.

2. **Small steps lead to significant progress**: Starting with manageable tasks and gradually building momentum helps overcome doubts and maintains motivation.

3. **Accountability is key**: Assigning accountability partners and conducting regular goal review meetings keep employees on track and maintain discipline.

Overall Assessment:

Transitioning from procrastination to discipline within XYZ Consulting has significantly impacted the organization. The initiatives implemented have transformed the company's culture. The measurable outcomes, including increased productivity and goal achievement rates, indicate the initiative's success. Though challenges were faced along the way, the company has learned valuable lessons that will help sustain the culture of discipline moving forward.

Moving past procrastination to discipline has empowered XYZ Consulting's employees to overcome doubt, take timely action, and achieve their goals. The company now enjoys greater efficiency and success, setting a positive example for other businesses facing similar challenges.

Now that we have examined the successful transition from procrastination to discipline within XYZ Consulting, it is important to highlight critical mistakes that should be avoided when implementing similar initiatives in your business. Based on the lessons learned from XYZ Consulting's case study, these mistakes will provide valuable insights and guidance for companies seeking to address procrastination and instill a culture of discipline.

Typical Mistakes And How To Avoid Them

1. **Ignoring doubt**: One common mistake is ignoring or suppressing doubt instead of confronting it head-on. It is crucial to be self-aware and acknowledge the presence of doubt in your life to overcome this,

2. **Accepting doubts as truth**: Another mistake is accepting doubts as reality without questioning their validity. Challenging your doubts and exploring evidence that supports or contradicts them is essential. This will help you recognize that many doubts are irrational and based on unfounded fears.

3. **Negative self-talk**: Many people fall into the trap of negative self-talk, constantly reinforcing their doubts and fears. Reframe your self-talk and replace negative thoughts with positive affirmations to avoid this mistake. Remind yourself of past successes and focus on your skills and capabilities.

4. Lack of clear goals: With clear goals, it is easier to avoid procrastination. Breaking down your aspirations into specific, actionable steps helps create a roadmap that keeps you focused and motivated.

5. Inaction and waiting for perfect conditions: Waiting for the ideal conditions or doubts to completely disappear before taking action is a mistake. Start with small, manageable tasks and gradually build momentum. Taking action is the antidote to doubt and procrastination.

6. Lack of discipline and consistency: Discipline is not an innate trait but a skill you can develop through consistent practice. Establishing a routine, prioritizing tasks, and holding yourself accountable are essential in cultivating discipline.

While there may be bumps along the way, staying committed to your goals and persevering will help you overcome doubt and conquer procrastination.

Now that we have discussed the common mistakes to avoid let's delve into the #1 piece of advice I have developed to help you avoid these pitfalls and achieve success.

My #1 Piece Of Advice

Understand the difference between Procrastination and Discipline.

Procrastination is **NOT** doing what you know you need to do because of how you feel about doing it. Discipline is **DOING** what you know you need to do, regardless of how you feel about doing it. You will fail if everything you do is solely based on your feelings!

Why? Because we are not always going to feel like doing what we need to do, but successful entrepreneurs do it anyway.

So, take consistent action towards your goals, even if it's small, even if you're unsure or don't feel like it. When you do, it builds momentum and will help you get beyond your doubt and fear.

To wrap up this chapter, I have created an Action Steps Checklist that will be a great reminder of the steps necessary to transition from procrastination to discipline. By following this checklist, you'll be well on your way to achieving your goals and realizing your full potential. Let's dive in and conquer procrastination together.

Action Steps Checklist:

1. **Recognize and acknowledge your doubt**s. Be aware of when doubt creeps in and how it affects your ability to act.

2. **Challenge your doubts by questioning their validity**. Look for evidence that contradicts or disproves your doubts and recognize that they are oftentimes based on irrational fears.

3. **Reframe your self-talk and replace negative thoughts with positive affirmations**. Remind yourself of past successes and the skills you possess that make you capable of achieving greatness.

4. **Set clear goals and break them down into specific, actionable steps**. Create a roadmap for yourself to follow, making it harder for doubt to hold you back.

5. **Start with small, manageable tasks and gradually build momentum**. Take action, as action is the antidote to doubt and procrastination. The more you act, the less power doubt will hold over you.

6. **Cultivate discipline through habit-building.** Establish a routine, prioritize your tasks, and hold yourself accountable. Remember that discipline is a skill that you can develop through consistent practice.

7. **Stay committed to your goals and persevere through the bumps along the way.** Doubts and fears may resurface occasionally but staying dedicated to your plans will gradually build the discipline and resilience needed to overcome procrastination and doubt.

8. **Embrace inspiration and let go of doubt.** Embrace discipline as your steadfast companion and commit to watching the magic unfold. The road may be challenging, but the rewards are worth the effort.

Understanding the link between doubt and procrastination is vital to positively changing your life. Exploring strategies that can help you overcome these obstacles is equally important.

In the next chapter, we will delve into the power of affirmations and visualizing success and how they can guide entrepreneurs toward building confidence and conquering doubt. Take advantage of these empowering techniques that can transform your journey – see you in the next chapter.

CHAPTER 9

THE DYNAMIC DUO: THE POWER OF VISUALIZATION AND AFFIRMATIONS TO MANAGE DOUBT

"Visualization is daydreaming with a purpose." - Bo Bennett.

"Affirmations are positive words that you speak that focus you on the things you want and the person you want to become." - Jerry Roisentul.

In this chapter, we will cover how to:

- Discover the powerful tools that can boost your confidence and help you overcome doubts and fears.

- Learn how visualization and affirmations can shift your mindset and create a positive belief in your abilities.

- Unleash the potential of visualization and affirmations to build unshakable confidence and achieve extraordinary results.

- Find out how engaging all your senses and emotions can make visualization and affirmations more effective.

- Discover the key to integrating consistent action with visualization and affirmations for lasting confidence and success.

Visualization and affirmations are powerful tools that can significantly boost confidence and help you overcome doubts and fears. Using these techniques consistently and effectively can shift your mindset and create a positive and empowering belief in your abilities.

Visualization involves creating a vivid mental image of the desired outcome or goal. By repeatedly visualizing yourself achieving your goals, you can build the confidence to overcome doubts and fears. This technique lets you see yourself as capable, reinforcing a positive self-image and reducing self-doubt.

Conversely, affirmations are positive statements repeated regularly to affirm and reinforce desired qualities or beliefs. By consciously and enthusiastically repeating affirmations tailored to address doubts and fears, you can rewire their subconscious mind, replacing limiting beliefs with empowering ones. Affirmations can help you focus on your strengths, talents, and past successes, building solid foundations for confidence.

One of the key benefits of visualization and affirmations is that they train the mind to focus on the positive aspects of one's abilities and potential. By consistently directing attention towards success and progress, you build a reservoir of confidence that becomes your default state of mind. This heightened sense of self-assurance becomes a catalyst for taking calculated risks, stepping out of comfort zones, and embracing challenges head-on.

To make visualization and affirmations more effective, engaging all the senses and emotions is essential.

When visualizing, you should imagine the sights, sounds, smells, and tastes associated with your desired outcomes. Making the mental image as accurate and detailed as possible makes it easier to believe in its possibility.

Similarly, when crafting affirmations, you should choose words that resonate with you and evoke positive emotions. For example, instead of saying, "I am not afraid of failure," rephrase it as "I embrace failure as an opportunity for growth and learning." This reframing technique helps to instill confidence while addressing doubts and fears directly.

Additionally, it's crucial to integrate consistent action with visualization and affirmations. Confidence is not built solely through thoughts and words; it also comes from taking proactive steps toward achieving goals. It would be best to pair your visualization and affirmations with specific action plans, breaking their goals into smaller, manageable tasks. By continuously taking action and tracking progress, you reinforce your belief in your ability to succeed, further boosting confidence and diminishing doubt.

Ultimately, visualization and affirmations can transform your mindset, allowing you to overcome doubt and fear and achieve extraordinary results. When consistently practiced, these techniques foster a sense of unwavering self-belief, resilience, and determination in the face of challenges. By incorporating visualization and affirmations into your daily routine, you can build unshakable confidence and unlock your full potential in business and beyond.

Now that we have explored the power of visualization and affirmations in boosting confidence and overcoming doubts and fears, I want to share a personal story with you of something that truly transformed my life and how it can transform yours. If you embrace this and use it, it will have a powerful impact on your life and business.

Over 20 years ago, my business coach introduced me to a powerful tool he wanted me to use. It was an affirmation statement different from anything I had seen in the past. So, being a good student, I reluctantly agreed to do it. I refined what I learned to make it my own, creating what I now call "The Goal Card." At first thought it was the dumbest thing I had ever heard. I was seeking ways to grow my income, and my business coach handed me a set of words to speak every day. Little did I know the power of affirmations at the time.

Hesitantly, I started using the Goal Card. Day after day, week after week, month after month, I faithfully repeated those words. At first, I saw no change in myself or my business. I almost stopped doing it because I didn't see results. But I kept on going because I didn't believe in giving up. And after about two months of consistent practice, the results were nothing short of staggering. The belief and confidence it instilled in me were incredible. This little tool taught me how to manage my doubts and fears, so they didn't manage me. As my mind strengthened, so did my business. The more I used the Goal Card, the more my business changed. It not only transformed my business but my entire life.

When I embarked on my coaching business, I lacked formal training materials or programs to teach from. However, I had the Goal Card. I decided to share this tool with my clients. And now, almost a decade later, I have received hundreds and hundreds of testimonies from leaders worldwide whose lives have been profoundly impacted by the Goal Card.

If you commit to using this powerful tool, it can truly bring about significant and positive changes in your life. So, what exactly does the Goal Card say? Allow me to share it with you. I will provide you with all the verbiage, explain its meaning, and share with you the most effective way to use it.

The Goal Card Verbiage:

"I am so happy and grateful for perfect health, unstoppable confidence, and a constant abundance of time, money, and freedom in my life.

I attract the right people, resources, and opportunities that will enable me to (insert your goal along with the target date you want to achieve it. I always find it helpful when it comes to the date to put "on or before," so it lets your mind know that accomplishing the goal earlier than the target date is also an option.)

There it is. Short and simple. Now, let me break it down.

__I am so happy and grateful__. It's great to start with this statement because no matter what difficulties or challenges you may be facing, there is **ALWAYS** something you can be thankful for. When you focus on gratitude for the blessings you have in your life, it begins to shift your mindset.

__For perfect health:__ My dad always taught me that if you don't have your health, you have nothing. He would always say, "What's the use of being successful if you're stuck in a hospital bed and can't enjoy it?"

Now, I understand that many people are dealing with difficult and potentially life-changing health challenges. So, saying "perfect" health may not feel right when you say it. I have always had the mindset that no matter how I feel, I want to focus not on how I am but on how I would like to be. Therefore, you can use words like "Improved health" or "Stronger health" as an example. Use whatever word you feel most comfortable with.

__Unstoppable Confidence:__ It always amused me when people I would coach could not figure out why they have little to no confidence in themselves or in doing something they need to do for work or their business. Yet, when I listened to them talk, all their words described their lack of confidence.

So, we need to speak what we want, not what we don't want. That's the reason for this little statement. If you want unstoppable confidence, then start declaring it and stop claiming that you don't have it. You will get what you focus on.

__And a constant abundance of time, money, and freedom in your life__. I recruited and trained a lot of people in my network marketing business. When I would ask them what things they would like to have more of in your life, this is what they would say 99% of the time.

They wanted more time with their family, more money so they didn't have to struggle to get by every month, and more freedom to live on their own terms.

When I started using The Goal Card, I knew I wanted that. At the time, I had no free time, was broke beyond words, and had no freedom to do anything I wanted. I started speaking these words, focusing on what I did want, and slowly, things began to change.

I attract the right people, resources, and opportunities. When I started using The Goal Card, I would say, "I attract the people." And boy, did I ever! I attracted everyone from everywhere. But that wasn't what I wanted. So, I changed it to "the right people," and wala…the right people started showing up! The power of our words.

I cannot tell you how many times people have called me and started the conversation with "You won't believe this," and go on to share a story of someone they had been following up with for months to no avail. Now, that person called them and told them they wanted to get together for a meeting.

I have seen the power of this statement alone work in my life. Once again, I focus on what I want, not what I don't want.

That will enable me to. This is where you put the main goal you are trying to accomplish right now. Whatever that goal is, write it down and then put "On or before" and the target date for that goal.

As an example: "That will enable me to hit my sales quota on or before Dec 31ˢᵗ." or "That will enable me to earn our company trip on or before Dec 31ˢᵗ."

Now that you have the framework and understanding of the Goal Card, I would like to explain how to turn this into a prayer card for my friends who would feel more comfortable with that.

You can word this however you want, but this is how several of my clients have done it:

*"**I am so happy and grateful to my heavenly father for perfect health, unstoppable confidence, and a constant abundance of time, money, and freedom in my life.**

Through the leading and guiding of my heavenly father, I attract the right people, resources, and opportunities that will enable me to (Goal and date)."*

Write it in a way that feels good to you. It's that simple.

Let me share a few quick tips with you to help you get the most significant benefit from this:

1) After 20-plus years of doing this and teaching it, it is best to focus the Goal Card on the most important goal you want to achieve now. Having too many goals all at once will confuse your mind. That does not mean you should not have multiple goals. Focus on your most important one to get the most significant benefit from The Goal Card.

2) Some people want to add all sorts of things to the Goal Card. Try to avoid doing that and stick as close to the framework I have given you as possible. Of course, you can make any change you want, but the more you change it, the less effective it becomes.

I'm sure the last question on your mind is, "How Do I Use The Goal Card?" Glad you asked.

I'm sure you all know about gravity. I can't explain all the physics of it, but I know if I jump off the roof of my house to show you how I can fly, you will pick me up off the pavement. That's how it works. The Goal Card has the same philosophy.

Your objective is to read the Goal Card **OUT LOUD** a minimum of 25 times a day to get the best result.

"Jerry, why 25 times?" The honest answer is, I don't know. After years of doing this and teaching it, that's the number where things begin to happen. Like gravity, I can't explain it, but I know that's how it works. This is one point you will have to trust me on.

People always ask me, "Do I need to read it out loud?" The answer is "Yes." The reason is that your mind needs to hear your words spoken out of your mouth. It makes a difference. So, don't think it, hum it, meditate on it. Say it out loud for maximum effect.

The other important part is that you can't just read the words simply to check it off your to-do list and get on with it. You must read the Goal Card with **FEELING** and **EMOTION** every time you say it. Don't just say the words; feel them. Visualize everything you are saying: See yourself with better health, living the life you want that more time, money, and freedom would give you. Feel it.

I learned years ago that you can't read The Goal Card 25 times in a row with feeling and emotion. That dies out about halfway through. The best way to do this is to say the Goal Card five times, five times a day, with feeling and emotion every time you say it. Minimum: 25 times.

I have clients who set an alarm on their phone to go off at 9 am, 12 pm, 3 pm, 6 pm, and 9 pm. Every time it does, they read their Goal Card 5 times out loud, with feeling and emotion. Whatever works for you, do it.

I can't express enough the impact this tool has had on my life and many lives worldwide. Some of you may be reading this and thinking the same thing I did when I first did this 20 years ago: "This is pretty dumb. I'm not going to do this." And you don't have to. But I would encourage you to try it before you say "No." If nothing happens, you are right back where you started from. But if something does happen, this can be a game changer in your life.

Let me share a few mistakes people make in visualization and affirmations and how to avoid them.

Typical Mistakes And How To Avoid Them

Based on the material covered here, one mistake most people make in visualization and affirmations is not using these techniques consistently. In order to see significant results, it's vital to practice visualization and repeat affirmations regularly. By doing so, individuals can reinforce positive beliefs and build their confidence. So, avoiding inconsistency mistakes is crucial to harnessing the power of visualization and affirmations.

Another mistake that people commonly need to avoid is engaging all the senses and emotions when practicing visualization. It's important to imagine the desired outcome's visual aspects and the associated sounds, smells, and tastes. By creating a vivid and detailed mental image, individuals can genuinely believe in the possibility of achieving their goals.

Regarding affirmations, a common mistake is choosing words that don't resonate personally or evoke positive emotions. Selecting words that genuinely connect with you and instill confidence is essential. Individuals can directly address doubts and fears by reframing negative statements and using positive language while building self-assurance.

Another mistake to avoid is solely relying on visualization and affirmations without taken action. While these techniques are powerful, confidence is also built through proactive steps towards achieving goals. It's important to pair visualization and affirmations with specific action plans, breaking goals into smaller tasks. By consistently taking action and tracking progress, individuals can reinforce their belief in their ability to succeed and boost their confidence even more.

By avoiding these, you can make the most of visualization and affirmations. These techniques can potentially transform mindsets and unlock a powerful sense of confidence and determination. With consistent practice and integration into daily routines, you can tap into their full potential and achieve extraordinary results in business and beyond.

Now that we have covered these common mistakes to avoid let's discuss my #1 piece of advice to ensure effectiveness and success when using visualization and affirmations.

My #1 Piece Of Advice

Believe in yourself and consistently practice visualization and affirmations to overcome doubt and fear. Make it part of your everyday life.

Action Steps Checklist:

1. **Decide on the main goal you want to focus on.**

2. **Write out your Goal Card with the goal and the "on or before" date.**

3. **Begin reading it out loud five times, five different times throughout the day, with feeling and emotion.**

4. **Journal your progress. Notice how you feel and any changes you see in your life or business.**

5. **Share this with your team and have them do their Goal Card.**

Now that you understand the power of visualization and affirmations in boosting confidence and overcoming doubts and fears let's explore how goal-setting can further enhance your journey towards success.

In the next chapter, we'll delve into the crucial role of goal setting for entrepreneurs and provide practical strategies for effectively setting and achieving goals. Keep reading to discover the key to managing doubt and fear while striving for your dreams!"

CHAPTER 10

GOAL GETTER: USING GOAL SETTING AS A WEAPON AGAINST DOUBT AND FEAR.

"Set your goals high, and don't stop till you get there." - Bo Jackson.

In this chapter, we will cover how to:

- Discover how setting clear and achievable goals can shift your focus from doubt and fear to purposeful action in your entrepreneurial journey.

- Learn how defining your vision and breaking it into manageable objectives can propel you toward success as an entrepreneur.

- Unleash your inner power and motivation by understanding how well-defined goals give you a sense of control and help you overcome uncertainty and setbacks.

- Master the art of goal setting with proven strategies like SMART goals, actionable steps, and regular review to stay on track and seize new opportunities.

- Unlock the secrets to a positive mindset and unwavering belief in yourself through visualization, affirmations, and the support of accountability partners, paving the way to your entrepreneurial dreams.

Goal setting is critical in managing doubt and fear, providing a clear direction and a sense of purpose. When faced with doubts and fears, you can often feel overwhelmed and uncertain about your abilities and the trajectory of your businesses. However, by setting specific and achievable goals, you can shift your focus from these negative emotions and channel your energy toward taking purposeful actions.

First and foremost, setting clear goals helps you clarify your vision and define what success looks like. This process involves carefully considering your long-term aspirations and breaking them into manageable objectives. By dissecting larger goals into smaller, more achievable milestones, you can effectively combat doubt and fear by having a clear roadmap to follow.

Second, goals provide entrepreneurs with a sense of control and empowerment. When faced with uncertainty and setbacks, having well-defined goals can be a source of motivation and determination. Entrepreneurs who set goals are more likely to confront and overcome their doubts and fears as they understand that progress toward these goals is within their grasp. This realization boosts their confidence and minimizes the impact of self-doubt and fear of failure.

You must consider specific strategies and techniques to effectively set and achieve your goals. It is crucial to ensure that goals are SMART (Specific, Measurable, Achievable, Relevant, and Time-bound). Specificity brings clarity to goals, measurability allows for progress tracking, achievability sets realistic expectations, relevance aligns goals with broader objectives, and time-bound deadlines create a sense of urgency.

Additionally, you should establish a systematic approach to goal-setting, which includes breaking down each goal into actionable steps and creating a timeline for completion. By carefully planning the necessary actions and timeframe, you can tackle doubts and fears related to progress and time management. Regularly reviewing and re-evaluating goals is also vital to ensure that you stay on track and adapt to any changes or new opportunities.

You can further enhance your goal-setting process by employing techniques such as visualization and positive affirmations, as discussed in the previous chapter, and accountability mechanisms. Visualizing the achievement of your goals helps you overcome doubts and fears by reinforcing a positive mindset and enabling you to envision a brighter future. Likewise, regularly affirming your capabilities and maintaining a positive self-image strengthens your belief in your abilities to confront challenges and achieve your goals. Having an accountability partner or joining a mastermind group can provide a support system that keeps you focused and motivated while ensuring you remain accountable for your progress.

In conclusion, goal setting is essential for entrepreneurs striving to overcome doubt and fear.

Let's look at examples I have created to help illustrate how you can apply these steps in real-life situations.

<u>Examples</u>

A young entrepreneur wants to start a clothing brand but is filled with doubts and fears about whether they have what it takes to succeed. By setting a goal to have their first collection designed and manufactured within six months, they can clarify their vision and define what success means to them. This goal gives them a clear direction and a sense of purpose, allowing them to shift their focus from their doubts and fears and instead channel their energy towards purposeful actions.

An entrepreneur who owns a small bakery is facing uncertainty due to the COVID-19 pandemic. They are unsure about the future of their business and feel overwhelmed with doubt and fear. They can regain a sense of control and empowerment by setting a specific and achievable goal to launch an online ordering platform within two weeks. This goal is a source of motivation and determination, as they understand that progress towards this goal is within their grasp. It helps combat their doubts and fears by providing them with a tangible action plan to adapt to the changing circumstances and continue serving their customers.

A serial entrepreneur who has experienced failures in the past is hesitant to launch a new venture. They are plagued by self-doubt and fear of failure. By setting SMART goals for their new business, they can boost their confidence and minimize the impact of their doubts and fears. Specificity, measurability, achievability, relevance, and time-bound deadlines help them create a clear roadmap for success. This systematic approach to goal-setting allows them to overcome progress and time management doubts.

Regularly reviewing and re-evaluating their goals ensures they stay on track and adapt to any changes or new opportunities, further enhancing their chances of success.

Entrepreneurs who desire to expand their business internationally may be faced with doubts and fears about entering unfamiliar markets. They can overcome their doubts and fears by visualizing their success in these new markets and regularly affirming their capabilities to navigate challenges. Envisioning a brighter future reinforces a positive mindset and helps them focus on their goals. Positive affirmations strengthen their belief in their abilities to confront challenges and achieve their desired outcomes. Additionally, joining a mastermind group or having an accountability partner provides a support system that keeps them motivated and accountable for their progress, increasing their chances of success.

Now, let's take a deeper look at how you can apply these strategies by using a case study that demonstrates the power of goal-setting in overcoming doubts and fears in entrepreneurship.

Case Study

Entrepreneur: Sarah's Sweets - a boutique bakery specializing in custom cakes and desserts.

Background:

Sarah started Sarah's Sweets as a home-based bakery business passionate about creating beautiful and delicious treats. As she progressed, doubt and fear started creeping in, as she felt overwhelmed and uncertain about the future of her business.

She realized that she needed a clear direction and a sense of purpose to combat these negative emotions.

Actions Implemented:

1. **Setting Clear and Specific Goals**: Sarah defined her long-term aspirations, which included expanding her bakery into a physical storefront and increasing her customer base. She broke these larger goals down into smaller and achievable milestones.

2. **SMART Goal setting**: Sarah ensured her goals were Specific, Measurable, Achievable, Relevant, and Time-bound. For example, by implementing targeted marketing strategies, she set a goal to increase her customer base by 50% within the next six months.

3. **Creating Actionable Steps and Timeline**: Sarah created a systematic approach to goal setting by breaking each goal into actionable steps. She made a timeline for completing these steps, ensuring progress tracking and timely completion.

4. **Visualization and Positive Affirmations**: Sarah regularly visualized herself successfully achieving her goals. She envisioned her bakery bustling with customers and receiving rave reviews. She also practiced positive affirmations to reinforce her belief in overcoming challenges.

5. **Accountability Mechanisms**: Sarah joined a mastermind group of fellow entrepreneurs, allowing her to have an accountability system. The group provided support, motivation, and feedback, ensuring she stayed focused and committed to her goals.

Measurable Outcomes Achieved:

1. **Increased Customer Base**: By implementing targeted marketing strategies, Sarah successfully increased her customer base by 50% within six months, per her specific goal.

2. **Expanded Bakery**: With a clear roadmap and the motivation gained from achieving her initial goals, Sarah was able to secure funding and open her physical storefront within a year, a significant accomplishment considering her initial doubts and fears.

Challenges Faced:

1. **Overcoming Self-Doubt**: Sarah consistently battled self-doubt and fear of failure throughout her journey. This required mental fortitude, self-reflection, and the regular practice of positive affirmations and visualization techniques.

2. **Adapting to Changes**: Sarah faced unexpected challenges and changes in the market, which required her to adapt her goals and actions accordingly. Regularly reviewing and re-evaluating her goals enabled her to stay on track and seize new opportunities.

Lessons Learned:

1. **Clear Goals Drive Action**: Sarah learned that setting clear and specific goals provided her with a roadmap and the motivation to take purposeful actions.

2. **Mindset is Key**: Sarah realized that managing doubt and fear required cultivating a positive mindset through visualization and positive affirmations.

3. **Accountability and Support**: Joining a mastermind group and having an accountability partner increased Sarah's focus, motivation, and overall success

Overall Assessment of Impact:

Implementing goal-setting strategies helped Sarah overcome doubt and fear, providing her with a clear direction and purpose. Sarah could navigate obstacles and achieve measurable outcomes by setting SMART goals, breaking them down into actionable steps, and utilizing visualization and affirmations. Establishing accountability mechanisms and a systematic approach to goal setting played a crucial role in Sarah's success. Overall, goal setting profoundly impacted Sarah's ability to set and achieve her goals, ultimately leading to the growth and success of Sarah's Sweets.

After examining the case study of Sarah's Sweets and her journey as an entrepreneur, it is essential to take note of the mistakes to avoid achieving similar success. By avoiding these mistakes, aspiring entrepreneurs like you can increase your chances of effectively implementing goal-setting strategies and navigating the challenges you may face along your entrepreneurial journey.

Typical Mistakes And How To Avoid Them

One mistake most people make in goal setting is not setting specific goals. Entrepreneurs may feel overwhelmed and uncertain about their direction without clear and specific goals. Avoiding this is important to ensure that goals are specific and clearly defined. That will bring clarity and focus, allowing entrepreneurs to know what they are working towards.

Another mistake that people make is their goals are not measurable. It can be challenging to stay motivated and track achievements without a way to measure progress. To avoid this, goals should be measurable, meaning there is a way to determine whether or not they have been achieved. This allows entrepreneurs to track their progress and celebrate their successes.

Achievability is another common mistake that people make in goal setting. Setting goals that are too difficult or unrealistic can lead to feelings of doubt and fear. Avoiding this is crucial to set achievable goals. This means by setting realistic expectations and considering your available resources and abilities, you can build confidence and minimize doubt and fear.

Many people need to set time-bound deadlines for their goals. Without deadlines, it can be easy to procrastinate or lose motivation. To avoid this, goals should have specific deadlines attached to them. This creates a sense of urgency and helps entrepreneurs stay focused and motivated.

Entrepreneurs can utilize visualization, positive affirmations, and accountability mechanisms to enhance goal setting. Visualization allows entrepreneurs to picture themselves achieving their goals, reinforcing a positive mindset, and helping to overcome doubts and fears. Positive affirmations involve regularly affirming one's capabilities and maintaining a positive self-image. This can boost confidence and belief in one's ability to achieve goals. Lastly, having an accountability partner or joining a mastermind group provides a support system and helps entrepreneurs stay focused and motivated.

By avoiding these mistakes, you can effectively navigate doubt and fear and increase your chances of achieving your desired outcomes.

Now, let me share my #1 Piece of Advice for this chapter.

My #1 Piece Of Advice

Prioritize self-reflection and self-awareness. By taking the time to deeply understand yourself, your values, strengths, and limitations, you can set goals that align with your true aspirations and abilities. This self-awareness will guide you in creating specific, measurable, achievable, and time-bound goals that are meaningful to you, increasing your motivation and commitment to achieving them.

I have created an Action Steps Checklist to summarize everything we discussed in this chapter and help you effectively set and achieve your goals.

Checklist

Action Steps Checklist for Goal Setting:

1. **Clarify Your Vision**: Take time to carefully consider your long-term aspirations and define what success looks like for you.

2. **Break Goals Down:** Dissect larger goals into smaller, more manageable milestones to create a clear roadmap.

3. **Make Goals SMART**: Ensure that goals are Specific, Measurable, Achievable, Relevant, and Time-bound.

4. **Create a Systematic Approach**: Break down each goal into actionable steps and establish a timeline for completion.

5. **Review and Re-evaluate Goals**: Regularly review and adjust goals to stay on track and adapt to changes or new opportunities.

6. Employ Visualization Techniques: Visualize the achievement of your goals to reinforce a positive mindset and envision a brighter future.

7. Practice Positive Affirmations: Regularly affirm your capabilities and maintain a positive self-image to strengthen belief in your abilities.

8. Establish Accountability Mechanisms: Find an accountability partner or join a mastermind group to provide support, focus, and motivation.

9. Take Purposeful Actions: Channel your energy towards taking purposeful actions that align with your goals.

10. Stay Persistent: Persevere through doubts and setbacks, maintaining motivation and determination to achieve your desired outcomes.

By following this action steps checklist, you can effectively set and achieve your goals, manage doubts and fears, and ultimately navigate your path to success as an entrepreneur.

In the next and last chapter, I will provide you with my final advice and words of wisdom, ensuring you have all the necessary tools to cultivate unwavering confidence in yourselves. So, please keep reading and allow me to guide you towards achieving your entrepreneurial dreams and finish this journey together.

CHAPTER 11

UNLEASH YOUR INNER CHAMPION: IT'S TIME TO TAKE WHAT YOU'VE LEARNED AND APPLY IT TO YOUR LIFE AND BUSINESS

"Success is not about the destination, but about the journey."

In this chapter, we will cover how to:

- Unlock your potential: Learn how to apply what you've learned in the book and create the unstoppable life you deserve.

Congratulations! We made it to the end. I am so proud of you for your dedication to learning. In finishing the journey you started by reading this book, I understand the importance of providing specific strategies and words of encouragement to help you apply what you've learned and create an unstoppable life.

I was always taught that repetition is the mother of learning. I mentioned some thoughts and ideas in the book several times in different chapters, which I did purposefully. The more you hear or read something, the more you understand the concept. It takes a person hearing or reading something an average of six times to gain a sixty percent retention. So, you will remember many of the concepts and ideas I shared much better.

I want to provide you with a final Action Steps Checklist to summarize all that we covered and give you an easy way to decide which ones you are doing well and which you need to work on.

Action Steps Checklist:

1. Cultivate a Growth Mindset:

- Encourage yourself to adopt a growth mindset by believing in your ability to develop through dedication and hard work.

- View failures and setbacks as opportunities for growth and learning.

- Emphasize the importance of perseverance in the face of challenges. Never, ever give up.

2. Embrace Collaboration and Networking:

- Actively seek opportunities for collaboration and networking.

- Attend industry conferences, join professional associations, and engage in online communities.

- Highlight the benefits of expanding knowledge, connections, and resources through collaboration.

3. Set SMART Goals:

- Set Specific, Measurable, Attainable, Relevant, and Time-bound goals.

- Break down your goals into smaller, actionable steps.

- Have a periodic reassessment and adjustment of your goals as needed.

4. <u>Cultivate a Supportive Environment</u>:

- Remember the importance of surrounding yourselves with positive and supportive individuals.

- Seek out mentors, accountability partners, and mastermind groups.

- Always be open to the value of guidance, motivation, and constructive feedback.

5. <u>Embrace Failure as Feedback</u>:

- Shift your perspective on failure by highlighting it as an opportunity to learn and grow.

- Reflect on your experiences, identify lessons learned, and make necessary adjustments.

- Remind yourself that successful entrepreneurs have also faced failures and used them to their advantage, and so can you.

6. <u>Develop Resilience</u>:

- It's essential for you to develop resilience in the face of obstacles and setbacks.

- Always see challenges as temporary roadblocks rather than insurmountable barriers.

- Practice mindfulness, self-care, and gratitude to build emotional and mental resilience.

7. **<u>Celebrate Small Wins</u>:**

- Celebrate your progress and recognize smaller milestones. The more you celebrate the progress and little victories, the more success you will have.

- Create the momentum, motivation, and sense of accomplishment that small wins provide.

- Boost your confidence to tackle more considerable challenges.

8. **<u>Practice Visualization and Affirmations:</u>**

- Commit to saying your Goal Card five times, five different times throughout the day, with feeling and emotion.

- Invest time visualizing the success you want to have.

- Create other affirmations that inspire you and speak those over yourself daily.

Following these steps, you can effectively apply your knowledge and create an unstoppable life.

As we end our journey together, let me share a few words of encouragement with you.

First and foremost, I want to express my deepest gratitude to everyone who purchased this book. Your support means the world to me, and I genuinely appreciate your trust and belief in my work. Together, we are embarking on a journey of growth and self-discovery, and I am excited to see where it leads us.

I wholeheartedly believe in you and the vast potential that resides within you. You have the power to achieve remarkable things and make a positive impact in this world.

My words and experiences can serve as a catalyst for you to unlock your true potential and live a life of purpose and fulfillment.

As we journey towards our goals, we must be wary of the naysayers who may try to discourage us. Do not let their negative voices deter you from pursuing your dreams. Remember, their skepticism does not reflect your abilities but rather a projection of their fears and insecurities. Stay focused on your vision and surround yourself with those who uplift and inspire you.

Let your life be a shining beacon of hope and inspiration to others. We are all interconnected, and our actions, however small, can create a ripple effect of positive change. Embrace kindness, compassion, and empathy, and watch as your light illuminates the darkness around you.

There will undoubtedly be moments during your journey when the road gets tough, and challenges seem insurmountable. I urge you to never give up on yourself or your dreams in those moments. Believe in your abilities, persist with unwavering determination, and trust that success is near. Remember, the most remarkable achievements often arise from the most challenging circumstances.

The most important thing I could encourage you to do now is take action. Implement the exercises discussed in this book with unwavering determination. Start small but start now. Formulate your daily affirmations, visualize your success, practice gratitude, and surround yourself with a community of like-minded individuals who will lift you up on your entrepreneurial journey

Lastly, I eagerly anticipate the day we can meet in person at one of my events.

The opportunity to connect with you, hear your stories, and witness the positive impact my words have had on your lives would be an absolute honor. Until then, let us continue to inspire and uplift one another from afar.

In closing, I want you to know that you have the power to transform your life and the lives of those around you. Embrace this journey with an open heart, unwavering determination, and unshakeable faith in your abilities. Persist, overcome, and keep pushing forward because the potential for extraordinary greatness lies within you.

It's time to let your light shine brightly for all to see!

With utmost encouragement and unwavering belief,

Coach Jerry.

ABOUT THE AUTHOR

From Suicide Attempt to Self-Empowerment: Jerry Roisentul's Story of Overcoming Doubt and Fear

When Jerry Roisentul hit his lowest point in life, he found the courage and strength to make a change and turn his life around. After going through a divorce, dealing with depression, and losing his business, Jerry was on the floor of his apartment ready to end it all. But instead of giving up, he chose to dedicate his life to helping others learn to master their mindset and create an unstoppable life.

Jerry is uniquely qualified to help struggling entrepreneurs overcome doubt and fear and reach their goals. As an in-demand Keynote Speaker, Certified Coach and Trainer with the Maxwell Leadership Team, Certified Behavioral Analysis Consultant and Mindset Development Coach, Jerry has traveled all over the world inspiring others to take control of their lives and create the life they desire.

Jerry lives with his son in California, and in his spare time, enjoys watching and attending sporting events, going to movies, hiking, and hanging out with close friends.

Made in the USA
Las Vegas, NV
21 December 2023